WINGS

OF CHANGE

How the World's Biggest Energy Drinks Manufacturer
Made a Mark in Football

KARAN TEJWANI

First published by Pitch Publishing, 2020

Pitch Publishing
A2 Yeoman Gate
Yeoman Way
Worthing
Sussex
BN13 3QZ
www.pitchpublishing.co.uk
info@pitchpublishing.co.uk

A CIP catalogue record is available for this book
from the British Library.

ISBN 978 1 78531 729 3

Typesetting and origination by Pitch Publishing
Printed and bound in India by Replika Press Pvt. Ltd.

CONTENTS

Acknowledgements. 7

Bull's Eye 11

A Tale of Two Clubs 20

Empire State of Soccer 28

The Leipzig Revolution 37

Plan A to Z. 46

Youthful Innovation 56

Kapital, Konzept and Kompetenz 70

Finding the Best of the Best 82

Comfortable with Being Uncomfortable 91

New York's Finest 101

Made in Stalybridge 111

Menschenfänger 120

A Promise to My Father 133

A Sporting Dynasty 141

Beyond Borders. 151

Continuous Improvement 159

Backlash 172

The Battle Within 183

Learning by Doing 191

Creating a Legacy 200

Spreading Their Wings. 209

Newspapers, Magazines and Online Sources 219

Books, Podcasts and Docuseries 221

ACKNOWLEDGEMENTS

IN NOVEMBER 2019, I watched a very good RB Leipzig team wallop Mainz 8-0. What impressed me was the speed and relentlessness of this team, who, even after taking a substantial lead, weren't backing down. A month later, Red Bull Salzburg lost at home to Liverpool in the Champions League. Despite the defeat, this diverse squad were exciting to watch, and it wouldn't have been a shock to see them win.

Those two matches stood out and were the inspiration for *Wings of Change*. This group of Red Bull clubs who are despised around the world – and rightly so – are doing extraordinary work on the pitch and have a sustainable model that will benefit them for years. Converting their short history into this book was fascinating.

No work of non-fiction is complete without the help of several people. For *Wings of Change*, there are some that I'd like to thank who have contributed to it. First, a huge thanks to Jane and Paul Camillin from Pitch Publishing who agreed to take the book on. Thanks also to Duncan Olner, who designed the neat cover.

Next, a special thanks to all the journalists, bloggers, writers and fans who spoke to me and contributed to this book with their intuition. They helped me aplenty with my research. In alphabetical order, they are: Abhimael Mela, Bastian Pauly,

Benjamin Siwale, Brian Sciaretta, Caio Vinicius da Silva Soares, Chris Medland, Derek Rae, Eric Friedlander, Filipe Rodrigues, Franco Panizo, Gerhard Reitner, Graham Ruthven, Guido Schäfer, Jack Brace, Jack Pitt-Brooke, Joe Goldstein, Johannes Höfer, Joshua Law, Kristian Dyer, Mark Fishkin, Matthias Löffler, Raphael Honigstein, Robbie Blakely, Ronan Murphy, Samarth Kanal, Stefan Schubert, Tom Scholes and Uli Hesse.

I'm grateful to Matt Ford and Constantin Eckner who helped me to better understand German fan culture and football in eastern Germany. Also, Tom Middler, Lee Wingate and Simon Clark from The Other Bundesliga podcast do an excellent job covering Austrian football in English, which is rare. They helped me greatly in many of the stories relating to Salzburg in this book. I must also thank Philipp Eitzinger for helping me grasp the complexities of the lower divisions of Austrian football.

I was also fortunate to get the chance to speak to Bradley Wright-Phillips (Los Angeles FC), Ernst Tanner (Philadelphia Union), Sandro Ingolitsch (SKN St Pölten) and Xaver Schlager (VfL Wolfsburg) and I'd like to thank them for taking the time out to talk to me. Their words provide plenty of insight.

I want to thank These Football Times and especially Omar Saleem. Without TFT, my love for long-form football writing would not have begun.

Heartfelt thanks to Al Diyafah High School in Dubai, without whom so much of what I know would not have been learned – their constant support, even when we are continents apart, is always appreciated.

Next, I'd like to thank my parents, brother and my family, whose care is eternal and always appreciated. Most of this book was written during the COVID-19 pandemic and lockdowns the world over – my family were a constant pillar of support during these times. I love you all.

Finally, I want to thank you, the readers, for getting hold of this copy. *Wings of Change* is the work of several months and the biggest project I've ever taken on. I'm so pleased to share it with you.

I hope you enjoy reading it as much as I've enjoyed writing it.

Karan Tejwani, August 2020

- This book was originally set to include details for the entirety of the 2019/20 season, but due to the COVID-19 pandemic, Salzburg's run in the UEFA Youth League from the quarter-finals onwards has not been included. The New York Red Bulls' revamped Major League Soccer season after the MLS is Back tournament has been excluded as well.

- All transfer data is correct as of August 2020.

BULL'S EYE

A QUICK scan through any of Red Bull's social media feeds tells you all you need to know about them. For a company that's grown to become the biggest energy drinks manufacturer in the world, their strategy to attract more consumers is simple: focus more on creating a brand that promotes a high-octane, high-energy, free-spirited lifestyle rather than promoting just the world-famous energy drink itself.

From snowboarding to skateboarding, surfing to kayaking and everything else that can be defined under the realms of extreme, Red Bull like to get involved. In many ways this is what has contributed to the success of their product and how they captured most of the market share in the energy drinks industry. The company has sold over 75 billion cans since their inception in 1987, but their focus goes beyond just the drink itself.

A cult drink in the modern day, its origins lie in Thailand, some 8,400 kilometres away from its current headquarters in Austria. It was here in 1976 that Chaleo Yoovidhya, a Thai entrepreneur, introduced Krating Daeng. The name literally translates to red bull, or red gaur, and it was sold in a unique 150 millilitre bottle that one would more usually find in a pharmacy. This simple formula of caffeine, vitamins and glucose caught the eye and taste buds of Thailand's many working-class people.

One of the primary ingredients in the drink is taurine, and this raised plenty of controversy and conspiracies. The word originates from its Latin form, Taurus, which means ox or bull and the initial conspiracies said that the taurine used in the drink came from bull semen. The organic compound aids muscle functions and boosts endurance. Myths were debunked immediately, and it was revealed that taurine was manufactured synthetically.

The fact that Krating Daeng was sold in a medicine bottle wasn't strange – at least not to the founder. Yoovidhya was the son of Chinese immigrants who moved to Thailand. In the mid-1950s, an aspiring Yoovidhya moved to the country's capital of Bangkok and tried plenty of different jobs, ranging from bus conductor to fruit vendor. The idea to sell pharmaceuticals then came about and, in 1956, he set up TC Pharmaceuticals, which manufactured antibiotics and cosmetics. It was here that Krating Daeng was born.

The energy drink market was untapped in the Far East at that time, with Japan's Lipovitan D being the only recognisable company. When that drink was first brought to Thailand in 1962, it caught the eye of many and that was Yoovidhya's inspiration. He made his version of the drink sweeter and more 'Thai-centric' to appeal to the local market and his packaging captured that too. In the foreground were two raging gaurs – a significant sight in rural Thailand as bull fights were famous in the region – while in the background was a yellow disc.

This eye-catching product was a great marketing tool right from the start, and its taste made it a favourite of many in the region. Over the next few years, Krating Daeng's popularity in Thailand would go from strength to strength, with its logos largely visible at fighting events – especially Muay Thai, the country's beloved combat sport. While the company's profile was growing and the drink was hitting high levels of popularity, it took an Austrian to enable the beverage to go international and become the superpower it is today.

Enter Dietrich Mateschitz.

The Austrian marketer and the drink were the perfect match for each other. Born in Styria, Austria, to a family of Slovenian ancestry, Mateschitz was raised by two primary school teacher-parents and it took him ten years to graduate from college. He left the Vienna University of Economics and Business with a degree in marketing in 1972 and worked for several companies such as Unilever and Jacob's Coffee in Germany. That was until he became the marketing director at Blendax, where he promoted daily utility products like toothpastes and shampoos in a job that took him around the world.

It was in Thailand where all that marketing experience would be put to good use, when as fate would have it, he would come across a famous energy drink, Krating Daeng. Just like it had done with so many others in the country, it captured his attention too. Mateschitz recognised how quickly it cured his jet lag and immediately started learning just how popular, marketable and profitable this drink was.

Fate would play a part once again. Yoovidhya's pharmaceuticals company was a licensee of Blendax, making it easier for Mateschitz to contact the creator of Krating Daeng. Immediately, Mateschitz flirted with the idea of making the drink go international and Yoovidhya was on board. Thus, in 1984, Red Bull GmbH was born. Mateschitz quit his job, invested $500,000 – the same as Yoovidhya – and each agreed to take a 49 per cent stake in the company, with the remaining two per cent going to Yoovidhya's son, Chalerm.

For the next three years, Mateschitz spent time making the brand more West-friendly, developing its image, its packaging and its marketing strategy before bringing it across to Austrian soil in 1987. The name of Red Bull was chosen to make it easier on the lips for the Western market, whilst the company moved away from the traditional medicine bottle that it had become known for, to a more captivating thin blue and silver aluminium can. Their catchphrase – 'Red Bull gives you wings' – was coined by a friend of Mateschitz, Johannes Kastner.

Kastner was running an ad agency in Frankfurt, Kastner & Partners, and being a close friend of Mateschitz, he agreed to do a service exchange with him due to the fact that the Austrian had little money. Kastner would help in the marketing side of Red Bull and, in return, Mateschitz would do some freelance work for Kastner's company. Coming up with the slogan was hard work for Kastner – with many ideas shunned, he advised his friend to find another agency to help out. That was until one morning, at 3am, Kastner came up with the now-famous slogan, and the rest is history.

The time before launch was also spent doing market research. Mateschitz hired a team to look into how the product might perform internationally – the results said it would fail. Nevertheless, the tycoon was undeterred; setting up an office in Salzburg, Austria, and commencing his venture. His target market was different too. Rather than aiming his product at the working class, he pitched it at youngsters, partygoers and adventurers who needed a tonic for their daily activity.

Perhaps the most innovative aspect of Red Bull's rise was how they created interest from scratch. Mateschitz told *Forbes* in 2005: 'When we first started, we said, "There is no existing market for Red Bull, but Red Bull will create it."' The creation began with sponsoring extreme sporting events. Mateschitz himself was a fan of such activities – his passions included flying, snowboarding and motocross so it was no surprise that he knew just what was needed in order to get their attention. Free sampling, spending next to nothing on TV or radio advertising and doing things on the ground itself – those were the company's core marketing values.

Red Bull's guerrilla marketing was effective, but they hadn't forgotten about their older, secondary market. In that area they sold themselves as a drink to help working males regain energy after a tiring day and cope with their workload. Additionally, they informed drinkers about the negative effects of alcohol and sold themselves as a worthy alternative. It was definitely a tactic that worked.

In 1991, Red Bull Flugtag (flying day) was born, an event in which competitors attempt to fly home-made, human-powered flying machines off a pier. A decade later, they launched Red Bull Crashed Ice, a competition that would see skaters race down a 535-metre racetrack. These are just two examples of how the company aimed to raise their popularity and engage with a potential consumer base. All these innovative strategies worked, more events have been launched in the years since then and many of them go across the world.

If it was anything that required liveliness, Red Bull were there and making themselves known. In a matter of years, Red Bull went from Austria to Hungary to the United Kingdom to Germany and then to most of the world. The interest was so high at the time of its launch in Germany in 1994 that the company failed to meet the demand for nearly one million cans a day.

However, the expansion wasn't plain sailing. Each market in each country had different requirements. Some may have been political while others may have been cultural – Red Bull had to adhere to it. The company's usual free-flowing, out-of-the-box strategies didn't work everywhere.

When Red Bull arrived in the United States of America, their people didn't take a liking to their small, traditional cans that were a hit in Europe, as they preferred beverages in bigger cans – the 500-millilitre tin was born there. Red Bull's link with extreme sports didn't go down well initially in some parts of Asia as well – in China, for example, they were banned in certain areas and new methods had to be found to sell the product, first to the mind, then in the hands. Over in Europe, France and Denmark believed Red Bull violated their food regulations. It wasn't until 2008 that Red Bull entered the French markets in its full, original form.

As the world became more technologically advanced, Red Bull adapted. First came their TV ads, mostly in the form of black-and-white cartoons that promoted the drink and its catchphrase. Once again, Kastner had a role to play. The voiceovers, tone, dialogues and animation were certainly a 30-second treat, giving the information the advert needed to give out and providing a small hit of entertainment. Most of them were worthwhile, but one particular ad in Italy – depicting four wise men instead of three visiting Mary and newly born Jesus in Bethlehem – caused problems. There have been plenty of other instances, with attempts at humour often being disregarded by viewers.

Even in the more digital era, where social media and rapid content-sharing has captured a youthful audience, Red Bull have succeeded. The Red Bull Media House, founded in 2007, focuses on everything Red Bull does, whether that's sports, their own music production houses (Red Bull Records, Red Bull Music), their film production house (Red Bull Films) or anything that has the logo of the two raging bulls with the yellow disc behind them. Boosted by their ownership and involvements in sporting and recreational activities, content never stops.

Their primary YouTube channel has over 9.43 million subscribers (as of July 2020) showing all the brand's activities in extreme sports. Their primary Instagram feed has 13.3 million followers, while on Twitter, they're on two million followers. Factor in the smaller accounts that are specific to a particular sport or activity and there is a large audience being reached on a daily basis. All of these feeds have a common denominator: fast, engaging content that immediately catches the eye. Another aspect worth noticing is how much of their content is videos and how many of them don't even focus on the product: the blue-and-silver aluminium can is rarely visible.

Red Bull's biggest success came in 2012, when Austrian Felix Baumgartner made the 'Space Jump'. The 128,000-foot jump which made him the first human to break the sound barrier was livestreamed on YouTube and drew over 2.6 million mentions on social media, making Red Bull Stratos the company's most prominent marketing stunt. This was the ideal definition of what they had been doing over the years: creating their own content, drawing in interest from around the world and, in the end, making an energy drink a world beater.

The company's attitude towards growth is simple: be clear and constantly communicate. Their famous catchphrase 'Red Bull gives you wings', signifying how the drink can provide a boost to daily life, is evident all the time, across all the methods of advertising. Their endorsements and sponsoring of events have made them a household name. Ranging from deals with celebrities and athletes, to their own creation, the Red Bull Flugtag, and the production of their own music, the constant aim of the company is to remind people of who they are and what it is they do.

The company is also intent on creating a positive image for itself, as is the case for every business out there. The 100 per cent recyclable aluminium cans show their concern towards the environment. An engaging, interactive page on their website shows just how they're trying to help the cause whilst painting a good picture of the company – the epitome of Red Bull: they make themselves hard to ignore.

While all of this has been happening, Mateschitz hasn't stayed too far away from the news. The founder makes rare appearances to the media, but recently for the wrong reasons. His political ideologies have been met with criticism in the past and his rare outspokenness isn't always welcome. As for Yoovidhya, the Thai businessman lived a low-profile life, away from media attention whilst still being a magnate who provided the initial idea for the world's most popular energy drink. He sadly passed away at the age of 89 in 2012 from natural causes. Worth an estimated \$5bn, he left behind an immense legacy. His family eventually branched out into different ventures, going into real estate and automobiles, but the thing the family name will be most associated with is Red Bull.

It's easy to forget that Red Bull's primary objective is to sell energy drinks and that they aren't just an urban high-octane marketing company. In the United States in 2019, they dominated, with the original Red Bull drink capturing 24.9 per cent of the market. Their sugar-free version is the third-most popular energy drink in the country, taking 6.7 per cent of sales. Sandwiched in between is Monster, their nearest competitors in the West.

Worldwide, their record of 7.5 billion cans sold in 2019 was a 10.4 per cent increase on their previous year and these were record-breaking numbers for the company. On their website, the company states their markets in certain countries grew significantly: India (+37 per cent), Brazil (+30 per cent), Germany (+15 per cent), and more. Red Bull is more popular than ever before.

Red Bull sit firmly at the top of the mountain. A beverage that's costlier than Coca-Cola and Pepsi is the world's go-to drink and they're not going to stop anytime soon. Over in Salzburg, Austria, their attractive headquarters building is shaped like two erupting volcanoes, representing energy. Nearby, sits Mateschitz's Hangar-7, the supremo's collection of historic aircraft and Formula 1 cars.

Not too far away from there is another part of the Red Bull empire. Much like the company as a whole, this one too is controversial, unique, futuristic and successful. In 2005, Red Bull took their involvement in sports to another level, taking Austria Salzburg, a football club, under their growing wings. Over the years, Red Bull's involvement in sport had grown, but this was another beast upon which they aimed to stamp their authority in the only way they knew how.

In a short period of time, things changed for the club that had over seven decades of history. The club, the colours, the crest, the culture and, of course, history itself were all changed.

Having been game-changers in many areas, football was now Red Bull's next venture and when they made their voices heard in the sport, people paid attention.

A TALE OF TWO CLUBS

IT'S THE 78th minute of a home game at Austria Salzburg. Franz Xaver Ager, commonly known as 'Schützei' has just made his way to the front of the players' tunnel in the compact Austria Stadion and in a loud tone begins his calling: 'Ratatatatatata,' he shouts, and he's answered by an even lounder shout, in unison, from the rest of the stadium: 'Austria!' This is a moment of pride, of remembrance and to the fans, of love.

This is a ritual religiously followed at most home games at Austria Salzburg, and it's always in the 78th minute as a mark of recognition. Thirty-three minutes into the second half, the fans pay tribute to their founding year, 1933, and remember a great Austrian footballing institution. SV Austria Salzburg – the phoenix club – were only founded in 2005, but their history goes back 72 years further, when the original Austria Salzburg were formed as a merger of two other clubs in the city: Hertha and Rapid Salzburg. Since then, they've had a stable history in Austrian and Continental football, reaching the country's top flight 20 years after their inception, making it to the UEFA Cup Final in 1994, where they lost to Inter 2-0 on aggregate. They established themselves as a solid team. However, things changed for them at the turn of this century, and that change influenced the club and affected Austrian football forever.

Red Bull, the rich energy drinks manufacturer who made the world take notice of them, were based in the same city, with their headquarters close by in Fuschl am See. Having become a renowned entity in extreme sports, football was their next target. Naturally, it occurred to them that starting local was the right move, and they did just that. However, no one anticipated that they would change the club in the way they did.

With Austria Salzburg struggling with financial issues as well as on the pitch, finishing second from bottom in the 2004/05 campaign and surviving in the top flight by the skin of their teeth, the interest from the beverage giant was a much welcomed one. As time passed by in the spring of 2005, the club's support was ecstatic that their club was going to be boosted by a major sponsor. Their chairman, Rudi Quehenberger, who was departing the club, raised expectations too. He believed the club was set to be in good hands with Red Bull and they had a bright future to look forward to. Even Franz Beckenbauer, the former World Cup-winning captain and manager and friend of Dietrich Mateschitz, was set to get involved with the project.

But then things began to turn sour. The traditional support of the club felt they were being robbed after realising that Red Bull were intent on being an owner, not just a sponsor. Many working at Red Bull's headquarters had no idea about the deal either. After the initial positivity, things went awry as Red Bull decided they wanted their own brand in football. Rumours were rife that the company wanted to change the club's colours and crest and the fans organised protests against the takeover. On 4 June 2005, a general assembly was held to insist the colours would remain. On 13 June, SV Austria Salzburg became FC Red Bull Salzburg.

The club's colours went from violet and white to Red Bull's red, white and gold; the club's crest was changed to highlight Red Bull's signature logo that was recognised the world over, and perhaps what stung the most was that they refused to acknowledge Austria Salzburg's history. On their website, they claimed the club was born in 2005, washing away 72 years of a football club that had been league champions six times and that had reached a Continental final just 11 years prior. Austria Salzburg were a club stripped of their identity, and it wasn't until the Austrian FA's intervention that a small victory was earned: they ordered Red Bull Salzburg to list 1933 as their founding year.

Commercialisation through name changing wasn't uncommon in Austrian football. Club names are often altered to include their sponsors and shirts are often plastered with logos. ASKÖ Pasching, a club founded in 1946, were known as SV PlusCity Pasching and FC Superfund Pasching, while SC Untersiebenbrunn were called SC Interwetten.com and SCU Seidl Software at one point. Austria Salzburg themselves had had a series of names, including SV Gerngroß Salzburg, SV Sparkasse Austria Salzburg, SV Casino Salzburg and SV Wüstenrot Salzburg, but when Red Bull decided to change the club in its entirety and dissolved its history, it enraged a large part of the Austrian football fan scene because of the depth of what they wanted to alter.

The fans' protests about changing the club colours were humiliatingly discarded too. Red Bull offered a small compromise to the angry supporters, saying the violet colour would be retained on the goalkeeper's socks at away games. That was the final blow; the fans of Austria Salzburg who had supported the club for decades were disappointed and, essentially, cast off. Fans that attended games in the club's former colours were ejected from the stadium and it was clear what Red Bull wanted: a legacy of their own. After dominating the energy drink industry, creating a market from scratch, they had the same intentions in football as well.

Red Bull's founder Mateschitz, disgusted the fans even further by stating bluntly: 'The red bull can't be violet, or else we couldn't call it Red Bull.' The alienated Austria Salzburg supporters decided to protest peacefully to avoid raising the possibility of Red Bull portraying them as antisocial hooligans. Fans were silent when they attended games, especially at the first match following Red Bull's takeover, against Mattersburg. Announcements over the PA system even reminded the capacity crowd of over 18,000 that they were attending a home game, but to no avail. The silence made noise around the country.

By the end of the match, they had gained more sympathy. The travelling Mattersburg fans revealed a banner that read 'stop mad cow disease' in reference to their rivals' new owners. Unsurprisingly, it was taken down, but it was a tiny victory for the fans' claims about the over-the-top commercialisation of the game. Over the next few months, protests, talks and disagreements would continue as this newborn, unaccepted Red Bull Salzburg was in the bad books of Austria's passionate football support. Football culture was a foreign concept for Red Bull. In the initial months after their takeover, fans watching the game at the stadium were treated to live commentary … over the PA system.

The initial months of Red Bull Salzburg were strange. The club, unofficially the most hated in Austria for what they did to Austria Salzburg, were lacking a plan and a clear identity. Led by Beckenbauer from a sporting sense, they were able to attract major sponsors including Adidas and Audi, but out on the pitch, the story was unclear. Under the management of Kurt Jara, Salzburg finished second in the first season following the takeover and, soon after that, he was sacked as Beckenbauer's connections brought in Italian legend Giovanni Trapattoni to manage the team with Lothar Matthäus as his assistant.

It wasn't just in the dugout that big names were present. Out on the field, Salzburg became a popular home for players who played in the Austrian and German Bundesliga. Present at the club at the time were former German internationals Alexander Zickler and Thomas Linke, both ageing and in the final years of their careers, whilst Trapattoni himself brought in a few more names from Germany including Niko Kovač, who had been plying his trade at Hertha Berlin. All of this contributed to a fair share of success over the next few years: Red Bull had the money, the players and the management to outdo their rivals.

'Die Mozartstädter' won the league that season in imperious fashion, their first trophy since the takeover. Salzburg finished 19 points clear of SV Reid in second place, with Zickler atop the scoring charts. Their power was unmatchable and Trapattoni was an example of that – there was absolutely no chance he would have moved to Austria had it not been for the high-end plans Red Bull had. The following season, a few cracks started to show. Salzburg finished second to Rapid Wien, who also toppled Salzburg 7-0 at their home ground, while there was a rift between Trapattoni and Matthäus.

Several factors caused the breakdown in the relationship between the pair: the signing of Ugandan defender, Ibrahim Sekagya by Trapattoni despite never having watched him personally infuriated many – Matthäus included – whilst the German disagreed with the Italian veteran's defensive style – for the World Cup winner, football was always supposed to be entertaining. In a scathing assessment of Trapattoni's work, Matthäus said: 'I always prefer a 4-1 over a 1-0. After all, the fans want to be entertained for their money and see as many goals as possible. Trapattoni will substitute a defender even if he is winning 1-0.'

From there, Trapattoni went on to manage the Republic of Ireland's national team in 2008 while Salzburg would go the Dutch way.

Meanwhile, just around four kilometres away in a tiny stadium behind a supermarket, were the passionate supporters of Austria Salzburg, the phoenix club created in 2005 after Red Bull's offer of the goalkeepers' purple socks. The fans that were disgruntled by Red Bull's almost sinful changing of their football club formed the new one, and although they don't have the same glamour or success as they did prior to 2005, the club is something the fans are incredibly proud of because it's something they believe in.

The support for Austria Salzburg, who have floundered in the lower divisions of Austrian football, is mammoth – far more than normal for this level. Most of their home crowds average around 1,000 fans, which is much larger than most clubs outside the top flight, and they get behind a common cause. The cheering, the customs of the 'Schützei', the cacophony of violet and white, and the firecrackers make Austria Salzburg one of the most special clubs in the region.

They joined the seventh tier of Austrian football in 2006 and ascended on a steady rise, making it as high as the second division in 2015. However, financial issues derailed their dreams of making it to the top flight, where they wished to face Red Bull Salzburg. Nevertheless, support remains strong for them and there is a grand optimism that they will reach the promised land in the near future. In the short run, the objective is simple: by the time the original club turns 90 in 2023, they wish to be debt-free. Rumours arose that they were willing to sell up to 51 per cent of the club in 2015, but those were wrong – this club only has one group of investors: the fans.

Austria Salzburg wish to be sustainable and not repeat the recklessness that essentially gave Red Bull the opportunity to capitalise in 2005. The goal of financial security in a few years' time isn't the most glamorous. The fans and the hierarchy want to see them win games and achieve great things, but only as long as it's done in a feasible manner that allows them to have a future to look forward to. The cash flow is still quite tight at the club, and losing money as well as talent following two successive relegations in 2016 and 2017 didn't help matters, but there is still plenty of positivity within everyone involved at the club.

A key figure of Austria Salzburg's renewed history is Walter Windischbauer, the former chairman of the club. He oversaw radical changes following their inception, namely with their stadium refurbishment in 2013 as well as the opening of their own artificial turf pitch, which the club often use for training and sometimes share with the local community for their use. However, things turned out badly for him as well and the general conception of him in people's minds lowered after a while. His misjudgements and frequent risk-taking didn't go down well and affected the club in many ways, including filing for bankruptcy and adding to their growing debt.

Now, Austria Salzburg are in a better position with around 900 members and chairman Claus Salzman leading the charge. The aim is still the same: keep the fans supporting, the club supportable, ensure the debt is gone soon and keep fighting to make it to the top division as early as possible. Just like the original club, the phoenix has seen its struggles too, but there has always been an air of hope and visions of a bright future. They also use their position in society as a fan-owned club for good, taking up volunteering opportunities in nations that need help, such as Gambia. In 2015, when the refugee crisis was at its peak, the club offered help to immigrants by giving them essential items to ease their worries.

Back at Red Bull Salzburg, there was an era of change. After Trapattoni, a triumvirate of Dutch coaches took charge: first, Co Adriaanse, who spurred Salzburg to regain the league title in 2008/09 in his sole season in charge; then came Huub Stevens, carrying on the club's dominance in the league and winning it again the following season – he lasted two years; finally, there was Ricardo Moniz, another who lasted just over a year, won a league title and their first-ever Austrian Cup and then departed in 2012. Despite the successes, there was still a belief that the project lacked the legs to last long in the future.

When Moniz came in, he was ordered to integrate more of the club's academy players, who they were developing in impressive manner with the aim of creating a self-sustainable model that would see them give their own talent a chance in the first team. Under his tutelage, players like Georg Tiegl, Marco Meilinger and Daniel Offenbacher, amongst others were all integrated into the senior squad. However, this model was still not going as planned due to the lack of footballing ideology and patience. It required proper football people to successfully carry through a big vision such as this one and, for that reason, while silverware was plentiful, satisfaction with the whole scenario was not.

For the fans of Red Bull Salzburg, there is no problem with Red Bull's influence. Whilst things weren't as good as expected on the pitch, off it the supporters adjusted to the seismic changes as time went on. Red Bull themselves tried to warm to their crowd, doing little things such as playing the 'Rainermarsch', an anthem that premiered during the First World War and is widely considered to be the Salzburg anthem, before home games and creating a more fan-centric atmosphere.

The fans believe that given the company's local background, it's only natural for them to get involved with the football team, as explained by Gerhard Reitner, a supporter since 1988 and regular season ticket holder since 2014: 'Red Bull is based here in Austria. Didi Mateschitz pays his taxes here in Austria. Here in the high-tax country of Austria he pays an estimated €300-350m in taxes per year, even though it would be easy for him to emigrate to Switzerland or any other tax haven. Red Bull is a good employer and is well established here in the region. As long as this is the case, Red Bull Salzburg will have popular support, especially here in their home city.'

It wasn't until the summer of 2012 and the arrival of Ralf Rangnick that everything changed for Red Bull Salzburg as well as the other projects Red Bull were involved in from a footballing standpoint. A football club and group with lofty ambitions needed shrewd people who knew the game, and Rangnick fitted that bill. If there was one person that could make Red Bull's voice heard, it was Rangnick, and he did just what was expected of him.

Reference:
Fieldsend, D., *The European Game: The Secrets of European Football Success*, Arena Sport, June 2017

EMPIRE STATE OF SOCCER

NEW YORK attracts attention. As one of the most popular cities in the world, when any event descends upon the Big Apple, it has a high profile. That stretches into sport as well, where any New York outfit is widely recognised. The Knicks in NBA (National Basketball Association) haven't won a championship in nearly five decades, while over in MLB (Major League Baseball), the Yankees haven't won the World Series since 2009. Yet, these two teams are amongst the most prevalent sporting institutions anywhere in the world for their history and locale. Merely a mention of the city breeds curiosity, and that law applies to soccer as well.

In 1996, amidst the boom of soccer in the States following the creation of MLS (Major League Soccer) and success of the World Cup two years prior, the New York/New Jersey MetroStars were one of the ten teams to take part in revamped professional league. New York was the biggest market in America, and it was essential that the city had a team as it looked to make the world take notice of its growth in what had been, until then, a sport not normally associated with the country. Joining them were other major cities: Los Angeles, Colorado, Tampa Bay, Dallas, Kansas and more, and in this surge of growth, big-name players and coaches joined the league as well.

The New York team's name was chosen in reference to the MetroMedia Group, the company owned by John Kluge and Stuart Subotnik, who were also the owners of the club. Initially, they were to be known as Empire Soccer Club, but that idea was rejected. Roberto Donadoni, who had been part of the Italy squad that reached the World Cup Final two years earlier, was one of the league's first stars, joining the MetroStars. Over the next few years, this was the team expected to top the charts each season – and there was reason to back them. However, this was a team that never did what was expected of them. Right from the start in their first-ever home game in MLS, when former Juventus defender Nicola Caricola scored a late own-goal to cost them a victory against New England Revolution, there was believed to be a curse surrounding them.

At that point, they were a struggling metropolitan team in a city that saw its other teams in other sports doing relatively well. They were playing in a stadium shared with NFL (National Football League)outfit, New York Giants, who were riding strongly in the east. Big names followed, including former Portugal coach Carlos Queiroz and World Cup winner Lothar Matthäus, but both proved to be underwhelming additions. Bob Bradley joined as manager in 2003 and he took them to the US Open Cup Final as well as the league play-offs, but the team faltered there as well. Eventually, the club would become MetroStars, dropping the name of the region they were in – a rare move in American sports. In the first few years of their existence, the MetroStars had flattered to deceive, but all that was set to change when there was interest from afar.

In 2006, Red Bull, who had made waves in football with their takeover and subsequent changing of Red Bull Salzburg a year earlier, were intent on doing the same across the Atlantic. This was a project Dietrich Mateschitz took a major interest in. For him, it was a chance to market the world-famous drink to over 18 million Americans who played the game as well as the 60 million around the country who followed it at the time. He, just like many others, recognised the potential soccer had in the States and was keen to exploit it. Having already established one club in Europe, targeting North America was an ideal step and seeing that statistical results pointed towards economic growth for both league and company, it made perfect sense to make the jump.

The Austrian company were initially keen on starting a new franchise altogether in New York; however, after learning the high costs of planning and managing as well as the stadium expenses, that idea was discarded. The process of starting a new franchise in America comes with plenty of obstacles. From assembling a squad to bringing together a coaching staff, plenty of work is involved and after avoiding this in Salzburg, Red Bull were keen on doing the same in New York. Instead, they took over the MetroStars, paying a reported $100m fee to Anschutz Entertainment Group (AEG), the company that operated the club, and negotiating the usual: changing the club's colours, crest and giving it a new identity – the Red Bull identity. The New York Red Bulls were born.

Reaction to the move was mixed. On the negative side, there was the feeling that, despite never having won a title in a decade of their existence, they wanted to have some authentic history of their own and that they would become overly corporate, as had been the case some 4,100 miles east in Salzburg one year prior. Many fans took a particular dislike towards the new crest, feeling that they were merely a promotional tool for an energy drink rather than a football club. Whatever negatives there were, though, were slightly put aside by MLS's young history as a professional league. In Europe, the idea of changing a club's identity was resisted because of clubs having a vast background; however in America, there wasn't too much of a protest due to their youth.

A key aspect of the positivity towards the Red Bull takeover of MetroStars was the eagerness to complete the stadium project. Since 2000, the MetroStars had aimed to build a soccer-only stadium, rather than share the Giants Stadium. Most of the time, the 80,000-capacity Giants Stadium (now known as MetLife Stadium), would only have about 15,000 fans inside for MetroStars' home games, creating a dull atmosphere. The venue was despised by the fans, and the fact that this was primarily an American football stadium didn't help matters. The club paid over $100,000 to the New Jersey Sports and Exposition Authority to use the stadium, but its playing surface was usually in poor condition, it was artificial turf, not grass and the faded NFL yard linings were often distracting.

All in all, playing at the Giants Stadium was a bad deal, and AEG considered areas in Newark and Kearny, before eventually settling in Harrison, New Jersey. For a year after the Red Bull takeover, AEG still owned rights to the stadium, but after several disagreements, they were eventually sold to the energy drinks manufacturer. The main reason for this was that AEG, also an entertainment and concert producer, wanted to have a fixed stage in the stadium – something Red Bull were against. After buying the rights, they redesigned certain aspects of the stadium, bringing in Detroit-based Rossetti Architects for the project. They wished to have a European and South American flavour to the stadium, bringing the stands closer to the pitch, thus enabling a finer atmosphere on matchdays.

Ten years in planning, several delays, a change in ownership and an estimated $200m later, the 25,000-seater Red Bull Arena was finally opened for fans in 2010 – a major win for the owners, who had got the supporters on board after delivering what they had been wanting for a long time. This was something the MetroStars and their previous ownership couldn't deliver despite being involved for longer, and it really set Red Bull apart. Taking over in New York was a shrewdly assessed move – they knew the costs of starting a new franchise were unreasonable and they knew they could take advantage of the stadium situation surrounding the MetroStars. In the end, it all worked out well. Now, there was an acceptance that in the short time they had been in town, they had done more good than bad, and that was also backed up by institutional changes made by the club on and off the pitch.

Red Bull were keen on exercising the marketability of New York and, as a result, with their financial might, were able to bring in top international talent to support their fine local players. In 2007, Colombian star Juan Pablo Ángel signed for the club in a move that strongly appealed to the city's Hispanic and Latino population, which had drastically increased at the start of the 21st century. Players from South and Central America had represented the club before, but none had the calibre of Ángel, who had previously dazzled crowds in Argentina and England. His immediate impact, which included a six-game scoring run and 19 goals in his first season, was welcomed and he would become a hero at the club as well as the Red Bulls' first marquee player.

Three years later, the Red Bulls signed arguably the biggest player in MLS history in the form of Thierry Henry. A global superstar who was Arsenal's record goalscorer and had just won the Champions League with Barcelona a year prior, he was a signing that massively boosted the club's brand. Playing briefly with Ángel, his record backed up his status as his four-and-a-half-year stay at the club produced joyous memories. In 2012, Tim Cahill, another Premier League icon, joined. It was becoming a trend for the club to sign players to boost their profile, and for the players themselves a move to New York was desirable – not only for the handsome salary packages that were on offer, but for the fine lifestyle as well.

The Red Bulls showed a greater commitment towards top-quality local talent as well. In their early years, they had the influence of captain Claudio Reyna, who was a helpful figure to the upcoming Jozy Altidore. That has continued over time with players such as Matt Miazga and Tyler Adams coming through – all going on to play European football at the highest level and raising the reputation of the Red Bulls' devotion to development of their own.

However, one stark similarity remained with the MetroStars: crumbling on the big occasions. The first instance of that came in the 2008 MLS Cup, a competition which announced Red Bull's arrival on the soccer scene in America and gave fans optimism about the future of the project. On the way to the final, they got the better of back-to-back defending champions Houston Dynamo as well as an improving Real Salt Lake. Ángel was in top form and created a good partnership with Dave van den Bergh. Led by future Mexico and Paraguay coach, Juan Carlos Osorio, they had an unexpectedly good season. They weren't able to go all the way, though, losing to Columbus Crew 3-1 in the final despite a strong showing in the first half.

Seeing as this was the first time most of their players had progressed so far, there was faith that the silverware would eventually come. The next year, they earned the chance to compete in the CONCACAF Champions League, coming up against Trinidadian side, W Connection. The away leg finished 2-2, which was an acceptable result considering the tough conditions and travelling involved. However, the return leg was a disaster, as the Red Bulls threw away a lead and lost 2-1 in a shocking result. That tie was part of a terrible season which featured a three-month winless streak between May and August 2009 and resulted in the sacking of Osorio plus a change in coaching structure.

In June 2010, another damning defeat occurred, this time in the US Open Cup. Playing at home against Harrisburg City Islanders (now known as Penn FC), who play in USL League Two, which is considered the fourth division of soccer in the States, they lost 1-0 in extra time. The goal the Red Bulls conceded was scored by Ghanaian midfielder Dominic Oppong, who had netted just one career goal before this. Whether this was bad luck or whether this was 'the Curse of Caricola' – a phrase coined as a result of the unfortunate defeat in their first-ever home match – the bad run seemed to have no end. The Red Bulls would lose the 2012 and 2013

Eastern Conference semi-finals, both after strong first-leg displays. Just when they thought they had broken the curse in 2014, they lost the conference final against New England Revolution, then suffered the same result in 2015 against Columbus Crew.

Despite the frequent heartbreak, the Red Bulls fans take some positivity from the fact that their club has an identity – something they feared would be lost following the takeover in 2006. They've made the play-offs for 12 years straight, they've won the Supporters' Shield, the annual award given to the team with the best regular season record, twice in that era – once in 2013 and the other in 2015. Perhaps the biggest achievement for them is that they've done all that with one of the smallest payrolls in the league. In 2019, the New York Red Bulls were behind Houston Dynamo and Vancouver Whitecaps as the lowest-paying teams in the country. Amazingly, in 2015 when they won the Supporters' Shield, the Red Bulls had the lowest payroll in the league.

The disappointment, however, has continued. In the 2018 season, coach Jesse Marsch, arguably the brightest the Red Bulls have had since the takeover, had taken the team a long way. His side secured the best points total in MLS history, winning 22 out of their 34 league matches, but failed to reach the MLS Cup Final (although Marsch left midway through that campaign). When Marsch departed, he had the best record in club history – 76 wins, 30 draws, and 45 defeats. Since his departure, things have gone awry. The Red Bulls were knocked out in the first round of the play-offs the following year and manager Chris Armas, who worked under Marsch as his assistant, was under fire from the fans despite a positive start to his tenure.

He isn't the biggest problem at the club, however. Recent times have seen sporting director Dennis Hamlett – a largely respected figure in the Red Bull football cluster – underwhelm in the transfer market. In a bid to control the spending, there have been some uninspiring transfers while several players have been sold for far less than their estimated market values. This has caused some serious disillusionment amongst fans and it has shown. The average attendance figures between 2018 and 2019 dropped by over 1,400, with fans believing they shouldn't care for the club if the people involved do not either.

The issue of a lack of investment in the first team is a serious cause of frustration and there are notions surrounding why that is the case. The club can only work with the budget provided by the head offices in Salzburg, and one notion is that Red Bull intend on focusing more on their two European clubs: Red Bull Salzburg and RB Leipzig. Additionally, there is a belief that the Red Bulls in MLS are acting as a feeder club and that the league's single-entity structure, which means teams and player contracts are centrally owned by the league, thus limiting the financial profitability (and losses) of their team, results in Red Bull being unwilling to invest to the fullest.

To steady the ship and help maximise the MLS side's potential, Kevin Thelwell was installed as the head of sport in 2020. The Englishman was a coach, working at the academies of English clubs, including Preston North End, Derby County and Wolverhampton Wanderers. He was a key cog in the Wolves machine that saw them go from the brink of falling into the third division in England to establishing themselves in the Premier League, but now his new role across the pond is to make the Red Bulls a force in America once again. The disappointing MLS is Back tournament wasn't the start the franchise would've hoped for.

In their short history, the Red Bulls are a storied franchise. From cursed beginnings to disappointments when it matters most, a commitment to youth and a delayed but much-welcomed stadium move, this is a club that has done plenty. Now, how they manage the future is crucial. Bad decisions are inevitable at most institutions; however, how they are reacted to is just as important as the good decisions and it'll say a lot about the Red Bulls in the coming years. They have one of the best academies in the country, have a track record of producing excellent talent – from even before the Red Bulls era – and are consistent in that area. The important part is making use of those strengths.

THE LEIPZIG REVOLUTION

LEIPZIG'S FOOTBALL history may not be the most well-known, but the city played a vital role in the emergence of football in Germany. In 1900, 86 clubs founded the Deutscher Fußball-Bund (DFB) – the German FA – in the city, while the first-ever German championship was won by VfB Leipzig. In later years, Lokomotive Leipzig (the successor to VfB Leipzig), added two more league titles, won cup competitions and were the pride of Saxony, being the strongest and most eminent team in East Germany. However, more recent years supported the theory that Leipzig, and eastern Germany, was lacking in a football superpower. That was until 2009, when the face of football in the region was set for an uplift and German football culture was altered forever.

After making waves in Austria and the United States, Red Bull set their sights on Germany from around 2006. With a similar ideology to the previous two makeovers, Red Bull wanted to build their way up in one of the most popular football nations in the world. They looked at several locations around the country, from Fortuna Düsseldorf to 1860 Munich to fan-centric St Pauli, but all their proposals were rejected. This was a tough country to please as clubs put their fans first and knowing what Red Bull did elsewhere, they felt that selling the rights to their club would cause a negative uproar. In the end, the

Austrian company settled on Leipzig – and their motives for choosing them were threefold:

- Germany and the German Bundesliga were a far more appealing market than the Austrian Bundesliga and MLS. If Red Bull wanted footballing success as well as a chance to grow their brand, this was a better option. Dietrich Mateschitz was desperate to see a Red Bull team in the Bundesliga and to be involved in Europe's premier club cup competition, the UEFA Champions League.

- Leipzig was a city with a grand past but a stale present – they had a strong reputation but didn't have a team to represent them at the top level of German football – the Bundesliga. East Germany needed a change too; after the fall of the Berlin Wall, there wasn't much to celebrate in these parts as the best football was in the west. In 2009, the same year that Red Bull officially began operations in the country, the former East Germany's only football representative in the Bundesliga, Energie Cottbus, had been relegated, while the only major club near them was Hertha Berlin – some 240 kilometres away.

- In Leipzig itself, there was significant support from the local authorities. People were intrigued by rumours of Red Bull taking over and politically there was vocal backing from an economic perspective. There was also a stadium waiting for them: the 43,000-capacity Zentralstadion didn't have a permanent user after being renovated for the 2006 World Cup and this was perfect for Red Bull to capitalise on.

Red Bull's search for a club to take over in Leipzig began with the two city clubs, Sachsen Leipzig and Lokomotive Leipzig. It is known that they approached Sachsen, who were in financial trouble at the time, but the club, true to their fans and their principles, immediately rejected the idea. With Lokomotive, there hasn't been clarity over whether they were approached, but even if they were, the move was quickly rejected.

Red Bull then turned their attention some 10 kilometres out of Leipzig, to a village called Markranstädt, which once hosted Napoleon Bonaparte for an overnight stay in 1807, had a population of 15,000 people and an amateur football team playing in the fifth division. The club had around 200 fans at the time and wasn't exactly well known. Although they were really low on the German football ladder, they were willing to negotiate with Red Bull, who believed they could fight their way up.

Hurriedly, Red Bull purchased their playing licence, and everything changed in the Red Bull way: once again, the crest, colours and identity all switched, and they were in business. When Red Bull set up their projects in Salzburg and New York, they managed to change the names of the club, giving birth to Red Bull Salzburg and New York Red Bulls. However, German league rules prevent commercial entities from adding their names to clubs, hence, RasenBallsport Leipzig e.V was born – the compound word translates to 'lawn ball sport' and fittingly abbreviates to RB, the initials of Red Bull.

Controversially, they managed to dupe the 50+1 rule that has protected German clubs from external majority ownership and kept them in the hands of the fans for over 100 years. In the 19th century, the German working class founded clubs which were suitable for their hobbies – these included various sporting clubs, including football. These clubs became registered associations – or *eingetragene Vereine (e. V)*, as often seen in a football clubs' official names [for instance, Ballspielverein Borussia 09 e. V. Dortmund]. Until 1998, these clubs remained non-profit organisations, but that all changed when the DFB allowed clubs to farm out their football operations to limited companies.

The new rules emphasise the condition that clubs, or fans, retain a majority of the voting rights – 50 per cent plus one share, hence, 50+1. This means that private investors cannot put profits above the will of the supporters and ensures the game stays with the fans. Some clubs in Germany have been exempt from the rule, such as Bayer Leverkusen, Wolfsburg and Hoffenheim. Exemption is granted if it can be proven that the entity supporting them has been substantially involved with the side for over 20 years.

The Bayer pharmaceutical company have been linked with Bayer Leverkusen since 1904, while automobile manufacturer Volkswagen have been connected with Wolfsburg since 1945. They've also been heavily involved with the city for decades and are a major part of the people's daily lives.

Hoffenheim, in more controversial circumstances, have been backed by Dietmar Hopp, the founder and owner of software company SAP. Hopp has helped Hoffenheim make strides through the German league ladder, going from amateur leagues all the way to the Bundesliga in the space of 18 years, from 1990 to 2008. They've faced plenty of backlash, but stayed within the rules.

In the case of RB Leipzig, they were assisted by top sports lawyer Christoph Schickhardt (whose clientele included Hopp) and managed to circumvent the 50+1 rule. Leipzig control all the voting shares of the football team, which means the members do not control the club. They officially have just 19 members, all of whom are linked to Red Bull, either as employees or agents. The average fan cannot become a voting member of the club, unlike other clubs in the country where fans can vote at the Annual General Meeting. Instead, fans can become 'gold members' at Leipzig by paying a massive €1,000 fee for an adult, which still excludes voting rights. In contrast, the membership fee at Borussia Dortmund is €62, while at Bayern Munich it stands at €60, with fans having a say at both.

In every technicality of the 50+1 rule, what RB Leipzig are doing is perfectly within the framework, but opposition fans aren't pleased.

Nevertheless, the club commenced operations and began their fight to the top. With the financial backing they had, it was expected they would reach the Bundesliga within a few years. The project involved huge planned expenditure: Red Bull paid SSV Markranstädt €400,000 for their playing licence, had a budget estimated to be at €10m – more than double that of clubs at the same level in German football – and planned on spending about €100m on their way to the Bundesliga, including costs for moving stadiums as well as building a brand-new, state-of-the-art training complex. The purchase of the licence and Leipzig's subsequent entry into the fifth division also meant that they jumped seven tiers of the German league ladder – had Leipzig been formed as a new club, they would've been starting in the 12th division.

Involved in the deal was 40-year-old Holger Nussbaum, the former Markranstädt manager and managing director, a respected figure in the area – he was the one that called the shots at the club. He negotiated a deal that saw the newly formed RB Leipzig take 11 of Markranstädt's first-team players as well as coach, Tino Vogel. Additionally, German rules stated Leipzig would need at least four youth teams to obtain a playing licence. Markranstädt would keep theirs to build for their first team in the future. Instead, Leipzig would turn to nearby Sachsen Leipzig, who were in serious financial trouble and could no longer finance their youth department. After receiving their licence in June 2009, Leipzig were given a year to complete their youth set-up. Markranstädt initially acted like a reserve team to Leipzig before going their own way later on.

Unlike Red Bull's previous two ventures in football, this move was welcomed by many local people. A survey conducted by local paper *Leipziger Volkszeitung* found that 70 per cent of the citizens of the city were happy with Red Bull's involvements with football in the area, believing it was their best chance of top-flight football after years of inconsistency by East German clubs. Additionally, the head of the Saxon Football Association,

Klaus Reichenbach, was also open to the move, seeing as there would now be a long-term tenant for the Zentralstadion, which had just been used sporadically since being refurbished for the 2006 World Cup.

Red Bull were extremely careful in their handling of the task and wanted to leave no stone unturned. Working under strict conditions set by the DFB and in a country where fans have a loud voice, they were keen to avoid any errors that would cost them early on. An example of that came through Andreas Sadlo, a former player agent who was working closely with the club. German rules stated that an agent was forbidden from working in the hierarchy of a club due to the potential influence they may carry and the power the club may have when negotiating transfers. Immediately, Sadlo put an end to his career as an agent and was appointed as the chairman of RB Leipzig.

Working under him was Joachim Krug, Leipzig's new sporting director. Krug had previous experience at a similar club, Rot Weiss Ahlen, who between 1999 and 2006 had been intent on climbing out of the third division and playing in the Bundesliga, with help from cosmetics manufacturer LR International. For a brief period, the club were called LR Ahlen until their relegation from 2. Bundesliga in 2006, when the company withdrew its sponsorship. Despite that, Krug's CV was decent enough to get him the important role at Leipzig, and he made some positive transfers in his first few weeks at the club. For Krug, the pressure was on, knowing he had to get this right: 'We have to get on, everything else is nonsense,' he said in an interview in 2009. 'If we don't go up, I'll go home.'

In came players like Ingo Hertzch, a 32-year-old two-time German international who had previously represented the likes of Hamburg and Bayer Leverkusen in the Bundesliga. Joining him was former Schalke defender Thomas Kläsener and Lars Müller, a Bundesliga champion in 1996 with Borussia Dortmund as well as former Nürnberg and Augsburg midfielder. Although these players were ageing and hadn't been outstandingly successful, it was a surprise to see them drop down so many divisions to start off a new club. That was the pulling power RB Leipzig had and they wanted to use that to go as far as possible in as little time as possible. Krug also highlighted the importance of keeping Vogel as the club's first manager, believing that he could take them up with a squad, league and region he knew well.

So rushed was the process from acquiring Markranstädt, building a structure and a team and getting all necessary registrations done that when the season started, RB Leipzig's club office was a container next to Stadion am Bad, Markranstädt's ground that was to be used until their move to the Zentralstadion the following year. It was on 8 August 2009 in the Oberliga that the club got its first real reality check. If Leipzig and its people were comfortable with the presence and plans of Red Bull, the folks outside the city clearly weren't and in their first-ever league game against Carl Zeiss Jena, the opposition fans made it clear. In a heated encounter away from home, the fans threw objects on to the pitch, hurled abuse at the players and made their disapproval of Red Bull evident.

They drew that day, but protests continued elsewhere. More abuse, more banners, more disapproval, but the team weren't deterred in their objective. In the end, they earned promotion in dominant fashion: 26 wins out of 30 in the league, 74 goals scored, 17 conceded and a 22-point gap over second place. Playing mostly against amateurs and youth teams of second-tier clubs, this was an easy task for them. Red Bull were also learning from other experiences: no longer were they looking to promote their drink at every opportunity and engage fans outside of football; they wanted to create a culture revolving around the sport and were constantly learning.

The following season, they finally moved to the Zentralstadion, acquiring a ten-year lease and just like in Salzburg and New York, named it the Red Bull Arena. Their first game there was a friendly against Schalke, who had been runners-up in the Bundesliga the previous campaign. The purchase of the lease was assisted by film entrepreneur Michael Kölmel, whose company, EMKA Immobilien-Beteiligungs, had built the stadium back in 2000 – he was also involved in the club's negotiations with Markranstädt.

Now playing in the Regionalliga, the cracks started to show. Leipzig believed that with the money they had it would be smooth sailing, but that wasn't to be the case. No club can function properly if they haven't got the right minds working behind the scenes, and the next few months showed that Mateschitz certainly wasn't the right mind to run this project.

The Red Bull supremo hired Dietmar Beiersdorfer, a former German international who had previously worked at Hamburg, as the head of football across all of Red Bull's clubs and his first noteworthy decision was a big one. Vogel and Krug were gone in the run-up to the season and there was a belief that Mateschitz was having difficulty controlling the club. The next manager had his work cut out. Seeing as there wasn't a sporting director at the club – a major mistake by Beiersdorfer – all the issues, including handling the squad, transfers, public relations and overall control of all things football at the club fell to new boss, Tomas Oral.

Soon afterwards, Beiersdorfer rectified this by hiring Thomas Linke, who played for Salzburg in their early years, as the new sporting director, but his reign was short-lived as Mateschitz interfered and after a glass of wine with former Dynamo Dresden and Rapid Wien coach Peter Pacult, decided that he (Pacult) would control proceedings. Angered, both Beiersdorfer and Linke resigned from their roles. Despite their first season going to plan, having older veterans either as players or coaches wasn't always going to work out in the fourth division. Even though Leipzig beat the Bundesliga's Wolfsburg in the DFB Pokal, Pacult's work was unimpressive, and the club were clearly lacking any direction.

This was a rich club with an incoherent management and after a season where they finished fourth in the Regionalliga and where much of the blame could be put on the people in the suits rather than those on the pitch, a revolutionary was hired. Ralf Rangnick was brought in to change things not just in Leipzig, but down south in Salzburg as well. In Rangnick's first season, Leipzig won promotion to the third division without losing a single game and then again to the 2. Bundesliga in the following campaign. It was then that radical changes would occur, as Rangnick took on more responsibility. This was the push Red Bull needed, and when it arrived, it would change the landscape of football in Germany.

PLAN A TO Z

ON 19 December 1998, a lanky Ralf Rangnick made an appearance on ZDF's *Das Aktuelle Sportstudio*, a German late-night Bundesliga highlights show. Accompanied by a host and a magnetic tactics board, he was asked to explain the zonal marking and four-at-the-back system that he had utilised for much of his career. Confident, he gave a full analysis, explaining what it did, how it benefitted his team and went into the intricacies of a model foreign to German football. While the analysis of the style itself was good, the backlash that followed as a result of him challenging German football and the Bundesliga's backwardness wasn't. The common reaction was that Rangnick was just a 40-year-old coach of second-division side SSV Ulm – who was he to challenge the upper echelons of German tactics? Why was he going against the idea of a sweeper, the very role Germany popularised?

Although Rangnick later admitted he regretted going on the show, it gave an insight into his mind – ideologies that he has stuck by throughout his career and that have earned him the reputation of being the father of modern German football tactics. He may have been a manager at a second-division club at the time, but his knowledge had been developed and honed for the previous 15 years when he was still a player, picking up details from the best in the game and forming his own unique beliefs on how the game should be played. There are three moments in the early years of Rangnick's career that shaped his future in football: coming across the great Dynamo Kyiv teams of the 1980s; meeting Helmut Groß, a man he would learn plenty from; and the aforementioned appearance on national television.

Born in Backnang, a town slightly north of Stuttgart, Rangnick began his career with local side VfB Stuttgart, but failed to get past the amateur sides. Further experiences took him to England, where he played for Southwick whilst studying for a degree in English and physical education at the University of Sussex in Brighton – a stint where his debut saw him end up in hospital with three broken ribs and a punctured lung. His playing career never took off, but it helped him gain important experience. After picking up some coaching experience at SSV Ulm, he joined boyhood club Viktoria Backnang as a player-coach where he would meet Valeriy Lobanovksyi and his incredible Dynamo Kyiv side. The team were at nearby Sportschule Ruit for their mid-season training camp and played Rangnick's team in a friendly. As a defensive midfielder, the German had his work cut out.

Rangnick told Raphael Honigstein for *Das Reboot* about this clash, which was his football epiphany: 'A few minutes in, when the ball had gone out for a throw, I had to stop and count the opposition players. I thought there was something wrong – did they have 13 or 14 men on the pitch? That was the first time I felt what it was like to come up against a team who systematically pressed the ball. I had played against big professional teams before – and of course we lost those games as well – but they at least gave you a bit of breathing space, the chance to "put a foot on the ball", as we used to say, a moment's breather to calm things down once in a while. In the match against Kyiv, I felt constantly under pressure for 90 minutes. And my team-mates did as well. I always felt that there had to be more to this game than following your opponent around all over the pitch and, if necessary, all the way to the loo. As a holding midfielder, I would often get good marks in the paper if I had taken out the opposition midfielder, having had perhaps five touches myself. That never felt quite right. But against Kyiv it was the first time I sensed: this was football of a very different kind.'

Lobanovksyi's team would often visit the region for their mid-season camps, and every time they were present, so was Rangnick, learning, picking up notes and developing his own approaches. Soon, he would re-join Stuttgart, this time as a coach of the amateur sides, where he would meet Groß, a civil engineer with a similar thinking to him. Groß spent much of his life working behind the scenes as an advisor or scout and meeting Rangnick was just as crucial to him. They would work together as Rangnick combined his learning from his fledgling coaching career with Groß's '*ballorientierte raumdeckung*', an idea that combined aggressive pressing with zonal marking. Their plans went hand in hand and they would learn together, reviewing the work of greats like Arrigo Sacchi and Zdeněk Zeman, both of whom were weaving their magic over in Italy.

The relationship between the pair carried on for some time and, after Groß was appointed at Stuttgart to oversee the youth sector at the club, he made Rangnick head coach of the reserves. Groß wished to implement his philosophies at all levels of the club so that when younger players made it to the first team, they could have a sense of direction. Rangnick, still an emerging coach at the time, duly followed orders. Within years, the results showed, as Rangnick's Stuttgart team won a German youth championship, beating some of the best youngsters in the country and, soon after, the Swabian himself was asked to take over as the head of amateur football at the club. However, in 1994, after a short time in the role, Rangnick resigned after he was denied the opportunity to be the assistant to the head coach.

He then spent 18 months working at third-division side SSV Reutlingen, an insignificant role, but then made a seemingly sideways move to SSV Ulm. While all this was happening, there was a quiet revolution going on in German football. Volker Finke, the head coach of Freiburg, led his side to a third-place finish in the Bundesliga in 1995 with methods similar to those Rangnick (and Groß) were practising two divisions below. In 2. Bundesliga, Wolfgang Frank's Mainz side, who had a certain Jürgen Klopp at centre-half, were applying similar ideas. More people were starting to recognise the flaws in Germany's football mindset.

At Ulm, he earned promotion to the second tier in the summer of 1998 and while they were hotly tipped to go straight back down, Rangnick's side defied the odds. Their modern style earned praise as they went 16 games without defeat and that phase included the appearance on *Sportstudio* that defined the coach, exasperated others and earned Rangnick the polarising nickname of 'fußball professor'. Rangnick's appearance on TV didn't please many, including recently appointed German national team coach, Erich Ribbech: 'I'm disappointed by this exaggerated debate about tactical systems,' he said. 'For instance when, as happened on Saturday, a colleague [Rangnick] is selling platitudes on television in a manner as if the Bundesliga coaches were a bunch of dimwits.'

Ulm would end up getting promoted to the Bundesliga, but Rangnick wasn't there for the celebrations – his promotion came in March 1999 when he returned to Stuttgart, this time as the leader of the pack. The Swabian club were inconsistent, first with their results and second with their management, and Rangnick was the fifth person in the space of 12 months to take the hot seat.

However, this appointment and the subsequent events kicked off a trend in the manager's career. Rangnick, keen on implementing his theories, was unhappy with the way the club was run, believing that there were too many people involved in the process. He wanted things done his way, influencing even the tiniest of decisions such as where the team stayed during away trips or what they ate. A year later, he was gone, thanks in some part to a bust-up with the team's Bulgarian playmaker Krassimir Balakov, who was a revered figure in those parts. Rangnick's next job saw him go back down a division to Hannover 96.

He took the club back to the top flight after just over a decade of floating between the second and third divisions, but after just one season in the Bundesliga, where they survived, he left, once again citing issues with the management above him. Soon, he was in a job again, this time at Schalke 04. In Rangnick's first full season at the Veltins Arena (2004/05), he nearly won the championship, finishing second behind Bayern Munich, but six months later he left, once again blaming issues with the hierarchy. His last act was of defiance, going on a lap of honour around a packed stadium that appreciated his work – an act that provoked the club, who would let him go two days later.

The reason for these short stints was simple: Rangnick wanted to be his own man; he could be difficult to work with, but he was a visionary, which explains why he didn't do very well at certain clubs where he wasn't the head of the operation. He commanded a certain level of control and a certain level of technicality to his work. At a time where Germany was in adoration of the sweeper, he changed things. At a time where clubs believed a coach didn't need a big staff, he wanted more science, more technology and more information. His influence went beyond just football. Bernhard Peters, Germany's World Cup-winning hockey coach, took inspiration from Rangnick's zonal marking theories, believing that both football and hockey could take ideas from each other. The nature of Rangnick's work required a certain level of players and training, and that was given to him in his next move at third-tier Hoffenheim.

At the time Hoffenheim were a village club bankrolled by software magnate Dietmar Hopp, whose riches from his company, SAP, had seen them rise from the ninth division to the third between 1991 and 2006. At the first time of asking, Rangnick gained promotion to both the 2. Bundesliga and the Bundesliga and although he had help with Hopp's money, he did it in a unique, sustainable way. Rangnick made two important changes to Hoffenheim: one was to implement a transfer policy that only saw them sign young players that could develop in the future; the other was to build a state-of-the-art academy. Furthermore, he brought in Peters as the head of performance and Groß as his advisor as this 'blank piece of paper' – as he called it – was ready to create some history.

His changes were implemented in quick time: when Hoffenheim won promotion to the Bundesliga, his side was spearheaded by emerging stars like Demba Ba (23 years old), Carlos Eduardo (21) and Chinedu Obasi (22), amongst others. In the top flight, they were flying high. Detractors never took the club seriously for the financial might they had, but this project couldn't have been more profound. By winter, Hoffenheim were top of the league and more talent joined, including Luiz Gustavo (21). Rangnick's focus was on Brazilian players – he had four from the South American nation in his side at the start of the season. As the season went on and Hoffenheim started to gain more prominence, many of these young minds lost focus. Rumours were rife that there was interest in them from Europe's top clubs and they finished seventh.

The league standings weren't the worst, but considering the style they possessed and the start they made, more had been expected of the team. Playing with the speed and intensity that defined Rangnick's teams, they were mightily impressive. In a match against Bayern Munich in December 2008 at the Allianz Arena (which the home side won 2-1), many were astonished by the pace of the game with German publication *FAZ* calling for the inclusion of a match DVD in the curriculum for the German FA's manager course. Now, the top flight had taken notice. The next season, Hoffenheim finished 11th, which was a disappointing return, but the seeds were planted for an optimistic future.

However, that was Rangnick's last full season at the club. He left midway through the 2010/11 campaign after being infuriated by Hopp's decision to go behind his back and sell Gustavo to Bayern Munich. Later in the campaign, he took over at Schalke once again, leading them to the Champions League semi-final where they lost to Manchester United, and winning the DFB Pokal. In September 2011, Rangnick left Gelsenkirchen for a second time, citing exhaustion syndrome. He had been the team behind the team as well as the one leading it; he did too much, lived unhealthily and couldn't give his best.

Speaking to Jonathan Harding for *Mensch: Beyond the Cones*, Groß described the depth he and Rangnick went into to become what they are: 'In Germany, it's often said when head coaches have a philosophy, that the coach only has Plan A. He lacks a Plan B. What Rangnick and I have developed in a playing philosophy – we believe anyway – is a Plan A to Z. That means there can't be any problem that the game creates that we can't have an answer to. The solutions are, largely, different to others, but it's not like we have a gap somewhere. We've been doing it too long for that.'

After nearly a year away from the game, Rangnick looked to return in 2012, but rejected a host of English clubs. Then in the summer, a call came from Gérard Houllier, who was friends with Dietrich Mateschitz and was already on board to become their Global Head of Soccer, overseeing their development in the USA and Brazil: 'Hi Ralf, I'm just with Dietrich Mateschitz and we wondered if you were around. We're going to jump in a helicopter and visit you this afternoon.' That changed the destiny of Red Bull's football dynasty. At Hoffenheim, he had full control of one club. Now, Rangnick was overseeing two: he was the sporting director at both RB Leipzig and Red Bull Salzburg.

Once again, Rangnick put the emphasis on youth, efficiency, getting the right people for the right tasks and creating a sustainable model. When he arrived, the average age at both clubs was 29, with Salzburg just short of touching 30. Additionally, he believed they didn't have the right people working in the psychological and nutrition departments. Both were altered. Rangnick even stayed true to Red Bull's marketing ventures, telling Mateschitz in his first few weeks that 30-year-olds couldn't identify with the beverage and that a similar mindset needed to be applied with the playing squad. Within weeks, there was a complete overhaul at the club, and it showed.

The most important aspect was that there was now a similar playing style being applied at all Red Bull sides: something that gave their clubs wings. Rangnick's improved philosophy, according to him, came in four parts:

- Add maximum possibility to the team and act, don't react. You need to dictate the game with and without the ball, not through individuals.
- Use numerical superiority and let the ball run directly whenever possible, with no unnecessary individual action and no fouls.
- Use transitions and switch quickly. Try to win back the ball within five seconds with aggressive pressing. After winning the ball back, play quickly straight away, play direct and vertically towards the opponent's goal, surprise the disorganised opponent to get into the penalty area and shoot within ten seconds of winning the ball back.
- The more a team sprints to win back the ball, the greater the likelihood they will score a goal once they have won it back quickly.

This was to be the brand and, for that, he delved into the market for some unknown quantities. In Rangnick's first season, Leipzig gained promotion to the third division at the third time of asking and, as they improved, they started to attract more attention. More fans attended games, the media were intent on covering them and they were a hot topic in Germany. In financial terms, the books were also starting to look more positive as 'Die Rotten Bullen' got rid of some overpaid older players in favour of fitter, hungrier, younger talent. As Leipzig went upwards, two popular names, Joshua Kimmich and Yussuf Poulsen signed for the project in 2013 in a statement move.

Over at Salzburg, more youngsters started to join as they aimed to bring their average age down to around 24. Skilful players like Sadio Mané, Kevin Kampl, Valon Berisha and Péter Gulácsi joined in the first two transfer windows as Rangnick had two aims: bring in players with big potential who could provide adequate output for the short term; improve the players to a certain level where they could achieve a high sell-on value in the long run.

After years of inconsistency on the pitch for Leipzig and off the pitch for Salzburg, things were now streamlining. Boosted by the massive financial backing, Leipzig strolled through 3. Liga and in 2015/16, after two years in the second division, earned promotion to the Bundesliga with Rangnick playing the dual role of sporting director and head coach following the departure of previous full-time boss Alexander Zorniger. Fan interest was there as well: since Rangnick's first season at Red Bull, the average home attendance rose from 16,000 to 29,000 as eastern Germany took notice of the club's rise.

While the coaching was excellent, by no means were these promotions a fairy tale. Leipzig had a clear financial advantage over their rivals in the lower divisions – they spent over €53m on transfers alone between 2012 and 2016, while their advanced scouting system and links with their cousins in Salzburg proved to be beneficial.

Salzburg continued their dominance in the Austrian Bundesliga, but the Red Bull empire isn't just about what happens within the confines of a stadium. This empire, orchestrated by the genius of Rangnick, is the result of shrewd planning featuring a host of people with a similar ideology.

In 2019, Rangnick's role at Red Bull was altered. He was put in charge of overseeing the global side of the cluster, looking at how the teams in New York and Brazil are doing and integrating them with the two European clubs. In an interview with *The Guardian*, he explained what it takes to work with him: 'I am happy where I am but if any club wanted to speak to me, the question would have to be: "Can I be somebody who can influence areas of development across the whole club?" Otherwise you are only getting half of what I am capable of. If, after that, you can work together in a trustworthy and respectful way, then you are more likely to be successful.' Red Bull did just that, and as will be explained in the coming chapters, they are reaping the rewards.

References:

Honigstein, R., *Das Reboot: How German Football Reinvented Itself and Conquered the World*, Yellow Jersey Press, September 2015

Harding, J., *Mensch: Beyond the Cones*, Ockley Books, June 2019

Lyttleton, B., *Fishing in a Small Pond*, The Blizzard, Issue Sixteen, March 2019

YOUTHFUL INNOVATION

AT THE 60th edition of the Internationale Trainer-Kongress in Bochum in 2017, Ralf Rangnick spoke about the importance of youth in his club structures. The conference is a collection of Germany's football minds and Rangnick, who has been present several times, explained the ideology that drives him to promote young footballers and why he would rather give them a chance. He detailed several points and some of the standout ones were:

- Younger players have a lesser injury history and faster recovery process.
- Tactical differences: they have a greater will to acquire and implement tactical concepts.
- Motivational differences: young players want to get better; older players want to defend their position or get back to their previous best.
- Cognitive differences: the attention filter of younger players is much wider than that of older players.
- Social differences: the influence of external parties (fellow players, parents, agents, coaches) gives younger players a better understanding and aids in improving their social intelligence.
- High potential for market value enhancement.

Much of what he spoke about related to a difference in mentality and cognitive concepts between younger and older footballers – from handling criticism from the media or their own staff or team-mates to a sharpened desire to prove people wrong and further their own playing careers as well as a greater physical capacity to take on more tasks and clearly understand a playing philosophy. In his 45-minute speech, Rangnick displayed his clear fascination with working with youngsters and building his plans around them. That idea has worked hand in hand with the financial benefit he enjoys thanks to being employed by a multi-billion-euro company in Red Bull, as their academies across three countries and scouting network that goes across the world fits in perfectly with Rangnick's approach to football.

NEW YORK

The New York Red Bulls Academy, opened in 2006, was the first in the country to offer a no-cost programme and they consistently work to maintain an edge in player identification and talent development, which is a part of the reason they are almost always amongst the leaders in MLS in homegrown player progress. This track record has played a large part in the sustained success of the club's youth sector. The New Jersey area is a hotbed for talent in America – they've always produced players for the national team, with that record stretching to the days before Red Bull's investment. Players like Tim Howard, Jozy Altidore and Michael Bradley, who once formed the spine of the United States men's national team, can all trace their roots back to the academy.

The academy's philosophies are closely aligned with that of the rest of the Red Bull group. Taking a look into the models and systems of play, one will notice different formations and tactical approaches dependent on the coaches involved, but the underlying principles of direct, aggressive play in possession coupled with a high-intensity press when out of possession will be predominant across all teams. This is a key factor as it ensures a consistent pattern is maintained amongst younger players as they progress through the various age groups before potentially making it to the first team. Should they get that far, players know what is required of them and have a set philosophy in mind.

In the hunt for talent, the New York Red Bulls look for players who, while showing advanced technical and physical development, equally show strong character and aggressive play in the service of team principles. The academy has facilities to match or even exceed most MLS teams and its coaching staff and their methodologies only maximise a player's development.

There are select pathways in place at the academy, starting at grassroots level, that keep the club engaged and active with the soccer community in the Tri-state area (New York, New Jersey, Connecticut and north-east Pennsylvania). The pathways provide players with the opportunity to develop. If a player is identified at grassroots level, they will then have the chance to try out at one of the club's Regional Development Schools and receive supplementary training whilst also getting the chance to move into one of their pre-academy or academy programmes, furthering their progression at the club and opening the talent pool for the Red Bulls to pick from. The system is intricately connected and financially efficient and for those reasons it is regarded as one of the finest academy programmes in America.

In 2015, the New York Red Bulls II, dubbed the 'Baby Bulls' was founded – they serve as a reserve club for the MLS side. The aim of this club is to bridge the gap between the first team and the academy. It gives playing time to the academy graduates in the team, which currently plays in the United Soccer League Championship (the second-tier of American soccer), and also helps develop local talent for the first team. Additionally, the second-division side helps first-team players who are frequently left out of the 18-man matchday squad or players recovering from injury get some minutes on the pitch and build some fitness.

Florian Valot is an example of the importance of the secondary club. The French midfielder started his youth career in his native France with Paris Saint-Germain as well as the reserve side of AS Monaco, before moving across the Atlantic to attend Rider University in New Jersey on a scholarship programme as a member of their soccer team. In 2016, he joined the reserve team as a trialist and made an impact there, before getting a contract with the first team and becoming a permanent member of it.

New York Red Bulls II's victory in the 2016 USL Championship showed the strength of the academy – this was a first for a reserve side mainly bolstered by academy names. They eased through the Eastern Conference before a bumpy, but successful run in the play-offs took them to the title that year.

While Valot is a model for players within New York, Tyler Adams, a member of the roster that had won the USL in 2016, is the blueprint of an ideal Red Bull player. The midfielder joined the club in 2011, playing through all the age groups before making his debut for the senior team. As a youngster, appearances with the first team were sporadic, but his form in the USL made him a permanent fixture in the MLS from the 2017 season onwards. So good were his performances that he was seen as an ideal fit for European football, making the move to RB Leipzig in January 2019.

'We've been following Adams for a long time,' said Ralf Rangnick, who was Leipzig's coach and sporting director at the time. 'At 19, he was a key player this season for the New York Red Bulls, and he made his senior international debut for the USA. He'll be an immediate option for the midfield, and we're sure he'll take the next step in his development in the Bundesliga.' Adams is the player Rangnick envisions with this football model: developing the best youngsters from around the world in a similar manner, teaching them similar tactical concepts and opening pathways for foreign footballers to make it at the highest level in Europe.

There is also an influx of domestic talent from the New York Red Bulls academy into the first team. The current captain of the team is Sean Davis, a New Jersey-bred player who, in the 2020 season, became the first homegrown captain in club history. Additionally, he is joined by emerging players such as Brian White, Alex Muyl, Chris Lema and Kyle Duncan, who all began their careers with the club. They're still young and just how far they go remains to be seen, but the fact remains: the academy can still contribute heavily to the first team.

For most of this century, the Red Bulls' academy has been amongst the best in America, but while others have caught up in recent times in terms of players and access to facilities – namely FC Dallas, Philadelphia Union and the Seattle Sounders – the Red Bulls still have a strong reputation. They have an alumni that most clubs can only dream of and some players to look forward to who may just have a similar story to Adams in the future: John Tolkin, an 18-year-old defender who can also play in midfield recently signed with the first team; Dantouma Toure, a forward born in 2004 has been playing with the U-19s and Kenny Hot, born in the same year, has been playing at a higher level. Recent times may have been tough, but there is an optimism for the future.

SALZBURG

In 2014, Red Bull opened an elite academy for Red Bull Salzburg – the kind of which didn't exist in Austria at that point. Money-wise, they naturally had a big advantage, and they made full use of the capital available to them, creating a facility to compete with the biggest names in European football. The Akademie took 21 months to build, has seven football pitches (including one indoor) and hosts 400 young players: 200 footballers and 200 ice hockey players. Additional facilities include a gym, a coordination park and a video analysis suite as well as physiotherapy rooms. Located in a scenic location near the Eastern Alps, this magnificent venue has been the home to some of the finest Austrian talent in recent times and serves as an example of where Red Bull want to be in global football.

On paper, Salzburg aren't supposed to be this good. They have a population of just over 150,000 – the Austrian capital, Vienna, has more than 11 times as many. But, given their strong backing and excellent use of what they possess, they are one of the finest in the country and in Europe.

The organisation's insistence on technology is shown in some of the equipment available, namely, the 360-degree Soccerbot. This is a piece of technology which tests players' spatial awareness and technical speed through a series of games. It can also recreate in-match situations to provide analysis and objectively measure the cognitive abilities of players. As Rangnick has shown throughout his career, the use of modern equipment is of paramount importance across all Red Bull clubs, and that goes all the way down to the academy as well.

Additionally, some of the more intriguing pieces of technology are the anti-gravity running track which reduces a runner's body weight by 80 per cent as they try to sprint, as well as the Local Positioning Measurement (LPM) system, the most accurate tracking system in sport, which picks up data about positions of players as well as biometric information. Also, there is the IntelliGym, a video game-like training programme designed to improve memory and cognitive functioning whilst the academy is looking to create more room for virtual reality tools.

A vital aspect of training in the academy is helping players improve their motor skills and coordination techniques such as changes of direction, turns and jumps to stretch the body. Young athletes perform a lot of versatility training in the club's motoric park – an area with exercise elements to improve balance, dexterity, endurance and speed. That is all combined with video and data analysis, where the coaches and analysts are able to track changes in the development of young players.

Discipline is of the highest order at the academy. Players aren't allowed televisions in their rooms, but older ones can purchase their own, provided it's not more than 40 inches, while access to the internet after 10pm and using mobile phones or wearing hats in communal areas is prohibited. The strict rules ensure players are committed to the task in hand to the fullest. Salzburg also make certain that education is critical to a player's growth – the common belief is that the academy is '51 per cent school and 49 per cent sports'. Sporting progress is not the only reason the players are at the academy – they must be equipped for the future in more than one way.

At the Salzburg academy, there are over 100 people who are not involved with the football or ice hockey activities, but who make sure the youngsters are in the right state from a mental, emotional and physical perspective. These range from the head of innovation to the head of performance as well as educators, psychologists and more. They also cooperate with various educational institutions such as the Christian-Doppler-Gymnasium, where timetables are aligned with the players' training schedules.

The selection process at the club and subsequent training is of a very high quality. Red Bull also use their global network that reaches countries like Ghana, Brazil and the United States, amongst others, to bring in some international quality to their ranks.

Due to the restrictions put in place by FIFA regarding the transfer of international minors, they often form 'emotional links' with the family of a player who is underage and make it clear about how their child will progress at the club.

André Ramalho, who currently plays at centre-half for Salzburg's senior team, was a part of the network. He started his career with Red Bull Brasil, before moving to Austria in 2011 at the age of 19. The Brazilian eventually moved on to Germany to play for Bayer Leverkusen and Mainz, before returning to Salzburg in 2018.

The scouting network is well refined in Salzburg and their recruitment differs according to age group:

- Between the U-7s and U-13s, Salzburg only look at players in their region; that is anywhere no more than 45 minutes away from Salzburg;
- From the U-14s onwards, they look across the entire country as well as the bordering Bavarian region;
- From the age of 16, they go beyond the Austrian borders, where there are no restrictions for signing players from the European Union. Hungary's Dominik Szoboszlai is an example of this;
- Players from outside the European Union can only move after the age of 18.

The academy's former head, Ernst Tanner, who left his role in 2018 to join MLS' Philadelphia Union, spoke about the club's philosophy, telling Sky Sport Austria about the Red Bull DNA: 'You need a high cognitive ability to perceive things. Good decision-making ability. A fast action, a fast DNA plus a dynamic that you need in the best leagues in the world … You have to be a stand-up guy too. The players have to bring that with them from their own stance. You have to push your personal boundaries day in, day out, and explore them.'

Gerhard Struber, who was formerly with the Salzburg youth before moving to England with Barnsley, told Sky Sport Austria about the importance of communication in Salzburg: 'The behaviour of a player is best shown in the game itself. You talk to him about his game. You also have to discuss transparently and openly in which direction you want to develop together. What opportunities are there and what is necessary for this? Young players need a career plan. There are target discussions about personal and team goals. Then comes the evaluation: "Where do I stand after two months, where after four?' Relationship management and orientation are important for the player. You don't want to leave things to chance in development."

Like the Red Bulls in New York, Salzburg also have a feeder club, FC Liefering, who have spent much of their history in the second division. They provide a development route for young players – especially those from foreign nations – to settle into European football and gain some valuable minutes on the pitch in order to grow. Furthermore, they played a huge role in the youth team's UEFA Youth League (the European U-19 competition) success in 2017.

The Youth League win was the zenith for the academy. Along the way, Salzburg beat Paris Saint-Germain, Atlético Madrid, Barcelona and Benfica, becoming just the third club after the 'Blaugrana' and two-time winners Chelsea to claim the trophy. Leading the team was 40-year-old German coach Marco Rose, whose tactical innovativeness was appreciated by many across Europe. His tactical acumen had been renowned for several months and adding the Youth League after winning the U-18 championship in Austria the previous year was a prestigious honour. Rose had been at the club for four years and had overseen the rise of players like Hannes Wolf, Mergim Berisha and Xaver Schlager, who were instrumental in winning the tournament. Coincidentally, Rose's career started in Leipzig, his native city, with VfB Leipzig and he was a player under Rangnick at Hannover 96 as well as Jürgen Klopp at Mainz, who he cites as his managerial hero. More on Liefering and Salzburg's Youth League success will come later.

Locally, they've also been a class apart. Between 2013 and 2019, the three primary age groups – U-15, U-16 and U-18 – won 15 out of the 21 titles available to them and that includes 13 of the last 15 since 2015 and eight of the last nine since 2017. It's not just the financial advantage they have, Salzburg use their resources in the best way and have the results to match. If a player goes through their academy system, they are almost certain to have a career in football – if not in Salzburg, then somewhere else in the Bundesliga. St Polten, an Austrian Bundesliga club, have been massive beneficiaries from this –

they had seven former Salzburg academy players in their squad during the 2019/20 season.

Leading the academy at the time of writing is Frank Kramer, the former manager of Hoffenheim's second team and Germany's youth teams. In an interview with *Sportbuzzer*, he explained what makes Salzburg's academy one of the best in Europe: 'In Salzburg, everything adds up to an overall picture. There is a red thread that everyone follows. The philosophy is consistently lived throughout the entire association. This creates enormous synergies and makes training easier when everyone who is here or comes here has the same clear idea of football. This applies to scouts, coaches, managers and every single player. A further component is that the people who are here not only fit together conceptually, but also harmonise humanly. That's not something that can be taken for granted and, above all, it's not easy to achieve. And finally, the entire infrastructure is ideal for implementing the concept.'

LEIPZIG

Similar to Salzburg's academy, Leipzig also have a state-of-the-art facility with six pitches, one 1,000-seater stadium, which are used by both the academy players and the first team, and a boarding school. Located on the banks of the Elsterbecken, a river separating the academy from the Red Bull Arena, this venue plays host to some of the club's top talent; however, there is a major worry.

Unlike Salzburg or even New York, Leipzig's academy has not been very useful to the first team. Their youth teams haven't made much of an impact and, apart from winning the Northeast division in 2015, they have finished below the two Berlin clubs, Hertha and Union, as well as Werder Bremen and Wolfsburg. The club's youth sector hasn't been as fruitful for the first team and there hasn't been too much to boast about. Exceptions to this are players who have been signed from foreign academies. Factor in the point that the German Bundesliga is far more competitive and fast-paced that the Austrian Bundesliga or MLS and a pathway to the first team is difficult.

A major issue for Leipzig is that they don't have many top-level academies around them to feed off at U-11 or U-13 level, as is common with other big clubs in Germany. For example, Bayern Munich are often helped by the presence of Augburg, Regensburg, Nuremburg or even clubs across the border in Austria. The Bavarian club are the biggest in Germany and have few problems in attracting young players. Similarly, Borussia Dortmund are aided by Bochum, Bielefeld and Düsseldorf. Having talent mines nearby is of massive help to clubs, but Leipzig lack that.

After the fall of the Berlin Wall in 1989, the east of the country, where Leipzig are based, struggled in financial terms, while the west flourished, enjoying a *wirtschaftswunder* (economic miracle). This affected football, football clubs and aspiring athletes. East German football was in a long-lasting slump after that (as seen with the lack of presence of an East German club in the Bundesliga) and it continued for so long that infrastructure in the region deteriorated, with many clubs facing insolvency. This meant that investments in academies were no longer a top priority for most clubs in the region.

As a result of this downturn, players no longer had the motive to continue in this vein and were keen on going away to continue their growth because their hometown clubs no longer gave them the chance to get into the Bundesliga. This resulted in some of East Germany's best footballers finding their feet elsewhere. Maximilian Arnold, who was born in Reisa, Saxony, began his youth career at Dynamo Dresden but moved west to Wolfsburg, for whom he has played his whole career. Similarly, Jordan Torunarigha was born and raised in Chemnitz, the third-largest city in Saxony after Leipzig and Dresden but moved to Hertha Berlin at nine years old. Now 23, the defender has played for 'Die Alte Dame's' first team since 2016 and even represented Germany at youth level.

This has been a major contributing factor to Leipzig being unable to field any academy players in their first team – they have a hard time finding prospects when scouting matches in their region. The troubles have led to a new strategy in a bid to bump up their youth sector. The scouting network now looks for players outside of Germany who have a high potential and could make it to the senior team one day – some of their recent transfers have shown that. In 2019, they signed Spanish U-17 international Hugo Novoa from Deportivo La Coruña and he was joined by two Dutchmen in the form of right-back Solomon Bonnah from Ajax and winger Noah Ohio from Manchester City. Still in their teenage years, much is expected of them as RB Leipzig aim to boost their standing on academy prospects.

RB Leipzig are still a young club, only founded in 2009 and in the Bundesliga since 2016. They have a proven track record of working with young players and, with that in mind, they will certainly catch the eye of players from Germany and abroad. The first decade was spent building the club a reputation, the next will definitely see success not just at senior level, but in the lower age groups as well. Markus Krösche, the sporting director, revealed a five-point plan to *Bild* in April 2020 to improve Leipzig's academy's influence on the first team:

- **Philosophy**: 'We will stick to the basic principles of our game idea such as the high defensive line, fast switching, being courageous and creative. This idea should continue to be reflected in all teams. From the U-13s to the U-16s we want to lay the foundation,' Krösche said.

- **Squad guarantee**: three places in the first-team squad from the 2020/21 season onwards will be made exclusively available for academy players to train with the professionals, gain experience and impress.

- **Coaching**: coaches will be required to focus on player development instead of results. Krösche said: 'The evaluation of the coaches is not primarily based on the results on the weekend. It is about the development of the players and the speed of this development. The focus is on the players with the highest potential and their development.'

- **Expert training**: seminars and training will be made available for coaches to improve. 'If we want to train very good players, we must also develop our coaches to the highest level,' said Krösche.

- **Detachment from results**: coaches are encouraged to experiment in matches and focus on individual player development over the course of the week rather than match preparation. Krösche: 'Just as the boys are allowed to make mistakes on the pitch, the coaches should also be given the opportunity to try things out.'

Frieder Schrof, the former leader of the youth department at Leipzig who retired in 2019, is optimistic about the future. Speaking to *Sportbuzzer*, he said: 'Our Leipzig youth teams first had to be brought into the highest divisions [of their respective age groups]. When this was successful, the hurdle to the professional team was still too high, because highly talented young players formed the core of the first team … For the future, however, we expect a change. From our U-19s, we hope to see many make the leap to the professional teams. We also want to attract highly talented players at a young age as they mature into the professional age.'

Schrof joined the club in 2013 and oversaw many changes, including the building of the academy. He was replaced by a dual-leadership team of Christian Streit and Sebastian Kegel, who had been working with Leipzig since 2010 (Streit even played for the first team and scored Leipzig's first-ever competitive goal).

Red Bull's approach to youth football is unique, one that follows a fixed model that intends to be sustainable for the foreseeable future. That is combined with an acclaimed recruitment strategy for older players. With similar principles, Red Bull have formed a distinct ideology for scouting, development, training and management and that is the core of this empire that is certain to enjoy enormous successes in the future.

KAPITAL, KONZEPT
AND KOMPETENZ

IN FOOTBALL, Ralf Rangnick believes that there are three vital principles for a club to be successful: kapital, konzept and kompetenz. Inspired by former Bayer Leverkusen director Reiner Calmund's beliefs about succeeding in business which are capital, land and labour, Rangnick's version, which is altered for football, is a bit different but just as important if a club is to have a long-term, sustainable vision. He told German publication *Deutshce Welle*: 'If those three things come together, then you can be successful. If you have only one or two of them, then it is more difficult.' The German has successfully applied this to Red Bull, especially the two clubs in Europe.

Aided by the 'kapital' they have in abundance thanks to Red Bull, they have invested wisely and not only in the academy, but in the first team as well. Both Red Bull Salzburg and RB Leipzig have established a model for young players that suits their philosophy and sees emerging talents thrive at the club along with other players who have similar goals. The model sees them focus their money on youngsters only, adhering to Rangnick's theories on why youthful footballers are more suitable to work with (from the previous chapter) and it provides an indication as to why both clubs are so successful in their respective leagues.

Speaking to *The Blizzard* in 2015, Rangnick said: 'The difference between us, both Salzburg and Leipzig, [and other clubs] is that when we sign or scout new players, we are fishing in a very small pond. We are only interested in players aged between 17 and 23, as from our experience, when you are over 23, you are no longer a talent. If you look at other clubs and their development, you can see that players start their career earlier than ten years ago and finish earlier too.'

Following that method has certainly reaped its rewards for both clubs, as indicated by the talent at their disposal, the on-pitch success they have had and the value of their players.

RED BULL SALZBURG			
SEASON	AVERAGE AGE	SQUAD MARKET VALUE	RISE IN MARKET VALUE
2011/12	24.15	€36.28m	-
2015/16	21.65	€50.15m	38.23%
2019/20	23.56	€113.60m	55.85%

As seen from the table above, there has been a drastic increase in the total market value of the Salzburg squad over a period of time. The 2011/12 season was the last before Rangnick's arrival at Red Bull and the change in strategy, while the 2015/16 season was three seasons into his work that included their continued domination in the Austrian Bundesliga. Rangnick had also left his dual role of handling both Salzburg and Leipzig at the start of that season as he went into coaching the German side. As the years went on, Salzburg continued with their philosophies and, in the space of four years, the market value of their players doubled – even after the departures of Erling Håland and Takumi Minamino, two of their brightest talents, in the winter of 2020.

The Salzburg machine has been excellent, working with a diverse group of players from various parts of the world, bringing silverware to the club and maintaining a young, highly valued squad. Similarly, Leipzig have made exceptional progress post-2012.

RB LEIPZIG			
SEASON	AVERAGE AGE	SQUAD MARKET VALUE	RISE IN MARKET VALUE
2011/12	24.96	€326,000	-
2015/16	22.39	€35.30m	10,728.22%
2019/20	23.10	€630.40m	1,685.83%

Leipzig's progression through the divisions and coherent coaching has resulted in this massive burst in quality. In 2012, they were a side struggling in the fourth tier with some players that were too old and overpaid and some that were too young to perform consistently at their best. By 2015, the squad was more balanced, bringing in players such as Yussuf Poulsen, Marcel Halstenberg and Willi Orbán. They were bright footballers with good futures and that was shown as they entered the Bundesliga in 2016, finishing second, sixth and third in the full seasons since. In 2019, the squad was at its peak as the changes implemented by Rangnick have given them (and Salzburg) a plethora of talent, making their players some of the most in-demand in world football. Additionally, in the 2019/20 season, both Salzburg and Leipzig have fielded the youngest starting teams on average in their respective leagues – a testament to the commitment to their philosophies.

Salzburg have been immense beneficiaries of their success in scouting and finding the perfect players to suit their team. Between 2015 and winter of 2020, they made €276.5m in player sales and have a positive net spend of €205.86m. The idea of turning their coal into diamonds has given them the reputation of being one of the smartest clubs in European football and they have proven to be a self-sustainable outfit. Leipzig, meanwhile, have been rewarded for their continuous faith in youth as well and they have been aided by the prestige as well as the difficulties that come from playing in the Bundesliga, one of the toughest leagues in football. Many of their top players have been there since their and the club's younger days in the lower divisions and they are now valued highly. Working together has given the players as well as the club a high status.

Two examples of that are their leaders at the start of the 2019/20 season: Orbán and Diego Demme. Orbán joined the club when they were in 2. Bundesliga at the age of 22 from Kaiserslautern. He rose to become their captain and one of their best defenders. He is now estimated to be valued at €20m after signing for around ten times less. Demme, meanwhile, joined when they were in 3. Liga from Paderborn for €350,000. He was 22 at the time. Six years later, he left the club for Napoli for €12m. The move may have seemed strange as Leipzig were in a title fight and they had just lost their vice-captain, but to the people in the suits, it made perfect sense. Keeping Demme would've seen them go against their ideologies as his contract meant he would've stayed past the age of 30 – instead, Leipzig focused on clearing the way for others to come through, and in the process gave a small insight into their workings.

Back in Austria, the person in charge of Salzburg's recruitment is Christoph Freund, who has been with the club since 2006 and has seen them go from strength to strength. Starting in Red Bull's early years of involvement, the then 28-year-old did a lot of work around the team and their matches, helping in organising various aspects in the build-up to fixtures. He then moved to a more advanced role, becoming team coordinator as he developed contacts in human resources and legal work. In 2015, after Rangnick moved to Leipzig as permanent head coach, Freund was bumped up to sporting director and has continued to build on the solid foundations set for him. Now 43, he's a revered figure in the Red Bull set-up.

Freund explains the Red Bull 'konzept' to *Mirror Football*: 'We need speed, intelligence, good mentality, good character, [players need to be] fast in the head.' To add to that, Rangnick explains the similarities between Salzburg and Leipzig to *The Blizzard*: 'At both clubs, we try to play the same style of football and of course between the two clubs, we make use of synergies that can be developed out of those two factors.' Keeping players in the Red Bull cluster is important. Staying at either club, they can pick up the intricacies of what is demanded of them [as Freund explains above] and especially for non-European players, it's a chance to grow on the Continent.

Over the years, 19 players have transferred between Salzburg and Leipzig, mostly the best players from Austria moving to Germany. That illustrious list includes names such as Dayot Upamecano, Naby Keïta, Marcel Sabitzer (who moved to Salzburg on loan), Konrad Laimer and Hannes Wolf. Furthermore, some names such as Laimer and Wolf are Red Bull through and through, joining the club at academy level and progressing all the way to the German Bundesliga. The similar philosophies implemented in Red Bull's global network have also seen players join either European outfit from New York and Brazil.

These transfers have not been immune to criticism, however. Other clubs in the leagues feel they're at a disadvantage, while many have labelled Salzburg as a feeder club for Leipzig. The Austrians maintain their position, though, stating they are on their own path and cite the lack of activity between the two clubs since 2017, when Leipzig qualified for the Champions League (just four transfers) as an example. The fact that Håland, who was heavily linked to 'Die Roten Bullen', moved to Borussia Dortmund further strengthens their claim as they believe that the final decision in a transfer is down to a player and that if they wish to make a move to Leipzig, it is just natural progression, seeing as they play a similar style in a much more competitive and significant league.

The hunt for players to fit the Red Bull model has seen them heavily invest their money and attention in France. It is something they have been involved in and profited from in many ways since 2012. With France being the market for the finest young footballers in the world and later the home of the world champions, this is hardly a surprise. Right from the early days of Sadio Mané, who joined from Metz, and Keïta, who came from Istres, Red Bull have identified France as a place to find the athletic, intelligent players they are looking for. They have signed ten French players or players from French leagues and their scouting network is willing to go to great lengths to find the next big thing.

Gérard Houllier, who used to be in charge of Red Bull's global network, had strong connections in France and has good access to the country's lower divisions. Salzburg's former CEO Jochen Sauer spoke of the Austrian club's relationship with France to *The Blizzard*: 'We were always looking abroad. France was always an interesting market for Salzburg because it's one of the big European football markets but not as huge as the big four football countries [England, Spain, Germany and Italy]. We knew that this is one of the countries [from which it] could be realistic to convince a player to come to Austria. We had one advantage for this market that Gérard Houllier was the sporting director on the global side of Red Bull. His inside knowledge of France was good for us and made it easier for us to get enough information on players in addition to our scouting system. We focused on the second-division players in France because we knew that Ligue 1 weren't really focusing too much on them. From a financial point of view, they were realistic to get.'

Recently, they've often looked at Paris Saint-Germain's academy, plucking out several names just before they were given a chance in the first team or those who rarely featured for 'Les Parisiens'. The PSG alumni at Red Bull includes Abdourahmane Barry, Antoine Bernède, Mahamadou Dembélé (all Salzburg) and Jean-Kévin Augustin and Christopher Nkunku (both

Leipzig). Given the consistency of the French giants' academy, the standard required to play for PSG and the obvious quality of the players combined with economic benefits that may come as a result of the high increase in potential, thus the high sell-on value, it's a smart strategy that ensures Salzburg and Leipzig have players who are worthy of making the senior team.

Their far-reaching network has also seen them have a heavy influence in both Africa (more on that later) and Asia. Salzburg made a move for South Korean forward Hwang Hee-chan in 2015 after a lengthy scouting process. Although the initial years were tough, he is now a strong presence in the team and, at 24, is sure to have a good future. Similarly, Japan's Minamino was watched for over 18 months as he slogged at Cerezo Osaka. Just like Hwang, he struggled to settle in Salzburg, but the coaching of Jesse Marsch gave him a good run in the first team and he took full advantage. In January 2020, he moved to Liverpool, becoming the third former Red Bull player after Mané and Keïta to have moved to the Merseyside club since the arrival of Jürgen Klopp in 2016.

Klopp himself has been an admirer of the Red Bull model and after his side's clash against Salzburg in the Champions League in 2019 he told Freund that they were 'educating great players in Salzburg'. So impressed was Klopp by Minamino's Anfield display in September 2019 for Salzburg, where he scored one incredible volley and set up another, he was intent on completing the transfer as quickly as possible while the Liverpool players were pleased with his display when the two sides met in December that year, despite the then-reigning European champions winning 2-0 at the Red Bull Arena.

Players come and go, and a characteristic just as important as buying the right ones is having their replacements. In that respect, both Salzburg and Leipzig excel, looking several steps ahead, and nothing explains that idea better than Salzburg's 2019 and 2020 transfer windows. In the summer of 2019, the Austrian champions lost some of their best players, including

Moanes Dabbur to Sevilla, Xaver Schagler to Wolfsburg, Stefan Lainer to Borussia Mönchengladbach and Hannes Wolf to Leipzig. Despite that, they continued their fine form in the following campaign and performed better in Europe, placing their faith in the players that had been with them for several years, including Håland, Minamino, Dominik Szoboszlai, Enock Mwepu and more. When Håland and Minamino left in the winter, they had ready-made replacements in the form of Patson Daka, Sékou Koïta and Masaya Okugawa. They're still young, but given Salzburg's reputation in development, a lot of the names currently playing there will definitely make big names in the future.

The final aspect of Rangnick's three Ks is 'kompetenz'. Once again speaking at the Internationale Trainer-Kongress in Bochum in 2017, the German expressed the formula he applies to young players:

$$[\text{NATURAL BORN TALENT} + \text{ACQUIRED SKILL}] \times \text{MENTALITY} = \text{COMPETENCE}$$

Rangnick believes in the power of his work, the uniqueness he brings to the table and he's unafraid to do things that others are unwilling to take a chance on. For him, having a strong mentality is just as important as talent or skills obtained and that needs to resonate amongst his players as well. For a large part, that's been seen in the club's transfer policies as well, bringing in players with something to prove, who want to show that they deserve more than they are getting. Rangnick says: 'Our transfer policy is to sign players who are maybe on the second contract of their lives and they want to develop their careers step by step.' That carries forward to letting players go as well, where he believes if the move and timing is right and if the player sees the move as a natural progression in his career, he is open to leave. He adds: 'If you get the right offers, you have to let them go and have others in the pipeline.'

It's worth mentioning how a strong mentality and competence has made some of Leipzig's signings in recent years look like masterstrokes. At the time certain players were brought in, they were playing at lower clubs and not much was expected of them. That includes the likes of Marcel Halstenberg, who joined from St Pauli, Lukas Klostermann from Bochum, Ibrahima Konaté from Sochaux and Sabitzer from Rapid Wien. They were bought at a young age for a low fee and now hold esteemed positions and are essential to the Bundesliga club's first team: some are part of their national teams, some are considered leaders at domestic or international level, some sit atop the transfer target lists of some of the biggest clubs in Europe. This is competence: having the belief in one's abilities, fulfilling their potential and reaching the next level. Granted, Leipzig weren't in the best position either when these players were signed, but to take a group of youngsters on the basis that they would develop into something good was a calculated risk Rangnick knew was worth taking.

Two more players identified by this left-field approach to transfers were Yussuf Poulsen, who moved from Danish club Lyngby in 2013 at the age of 18 when Leipzig were in 3. Liga, and Emil Forsberg, who joined as a 23-year-old in 2015 when the club were in 2. Bundesliga. Both could've joined far more prestigious sides in other top flights but they joined Leipzig for two primary reasons. Firstly, it was Rangnick's persuasion powers and, secondly, it was Rangnick's belief that they could make it to a high level as footballers. Forsberg: 'You just have to bow down. He [Rangnick] is a very emotional guy and it's so easy to join in that emotion when he talks. He knows what he wants, wants everything correct in every small detail and that's what I love about him, because this guy is never satisfied. That's a big reason why the club is where it is today.'

Poulsen adds that the right mentality ensured he became a regular in the Bundesliga: 'I was never the greatest talent, to be honest. I was never the one that everyone said would become a pro footballer. I think I didn't realise until I was 17 or something that maybe I could make it! When I was 15 and we had the first national team pre-selection, I wasn't there, and there were 500 players from all of Denmark chosen from the 1994 age group. I had hoped more than believed that something would happen; it only happened very late. It was a challenge and when anyone said to me that I can't do it, I wanted to show that I can. Throughout my youth, there were always many players ahead of me, pushed ahead of me, chosen for the youth national teams ahead of me. It always gave me the motivation to try harder.'

In Rangnick's estimation, banking on Poulsen's mentality was well worth it, as he explained with his formula:

> **[NATURAL BORN TALENT (5) + ACQUIRED SKILL (6)] × MENTALITY (10) = COMPETENCE (110)**

Over in Salzburg, Upamecano was another headstrong character that Salzburg did their homework on. Signed in 2015 from France's Valenciennes, he struggled with injuries due to his immense physique – at the age of 15, he had the body of a grown man. Despite that, Salzburg paid €2m for the 16-year-old, swaying him away from Manchester United's interest before moving him on to Leipzig for four times the price just two years later. Now, he is one of the most in-demand centre-halves in world football in his early 20s and is sure to command a fee upwards of €40m.

The risk-taking policy has worked wonders in other areas as well. In 2019/20, Leipzig took a chance on three players: Nkunku, Patrik Schick and Angeliño. Nkunku's career largely stalled at PSG, as he fell behind in their unbreakable pecking order which featured players such as Neymar, Kylian Mbappé and Ángel Di María. Seeing as he fitted the bill, making a move for him was a no-brainer. Schick had shown his vast potential during the 2016/17 season with Sampdoria, but like

Nkunku, he too had failed to achieve anything of note in his next move to AS Roma. Angeliño, despite doing well at PSV Eindhoven, couldn't cut it at Manchester City and a move was arranged just six months after he joined the then-reigning English champions. All three had a huge rejuvenation. Nkunku was one of the Bundesliga's biggest creative forces; Schick was only behind Timo Werner and Sabitzer on the club's scoring charts; Angeliño was given a consistent run in the first team.

To ensure players' growth, Rangnick maintains a strict disciplinary policy. Younger players can easily have their heads turned by the increased attention, and while deflecting the attention is an impossible task, Rangnick and the clubs do their best to make sure players keep their feet on the ground, no matter if they're on the bench or starters for their respective national teams – and that stretches down to the cars they are allowed. Players over 24 are given the permission to own 'fast' cars, while those between 18 and 23 have to pick lesser models.

Interestingly, in 2018 when Rangnick was the head coach, he introduced a 'wheel of misfortune' for players who behaved irresponsibly. This helped dole out punishments in instances where players were late, used their phones during training or were overweight. The list of punishments included volunteering in the club shop, guiding stadium tours, helping the kit assistant, helping load the team bus with equipment for away fixtures, filling water bottles ahead of training, mowing the training pitches, serving food in the cafeteria, training one of the academy teams on a free day, pumping up and cleaning the footballs ahead of training for a week, buying small gifts for all of the club staff and, most embarrassingly, training in a tutu. Rangnick believed financial penalties were no longer viable and this method, inspired by then-assistant Marsch, was the best alternative.

For the best part of a decade, the three Ks of kapital, konzept and kompetenz have stuck around both Red Bull clubs and those principles have helped both Salzburg and Leipzig establish themselves as two reputable institutions in European football. The clubs are still young, but Rangnick, along with other key figures, has helped set them up strongly for the future, which is certain to be bright. As they strive for perfection, no stone is left unturned.

References:
Harding, J., *Mensch: Beyond the Cones*, Ockley Books, June 2019
Wilkes, P., *The Quiet Man*, The Blizzard, Issue Thirty-Three, June 2019
Lyttleton, B., *Fishing in a Small Pond*, The Blizzard, Issue Sixteen, March 2019
Fieldsend, D., *The European Game: The Secrets of European Football Success*, Arena Sport, June 2017

FINDING THE BEST
OF THE BEST

ON 18 January 2014, Bayern Munich visited the Red Bull Arena in Austria for a mid-season friendly against Roger Schmidt's Red Bull Salzburg. The Bavarians, reigning European champions and coached by Pep Guardiola, were looking to defend their European crown, and were expecting a routine warm-up game as they approached the second half of the season. While the German side may have seen this as a mere friendly, for the Austrians, this was an opportunity to shine, as they rarely got games this big. Both coaches fielded much of their strongest teams and on a pitch containing the likes of Manuel Neuer, Toni Kroos, Thomas Müller and Thiago Alcântara, it was a relatively unknown quantity in the form of Sadio Mané who stood out as the best performer.

The fiery Senegalese scored the opener, won the penalty which doubled Salzburg's advantage and then set up the third – all in the first half. He was unfortunate to hit the bar with a header in the second period, but in the 83 minutes that he spent on the pitch, he was a constant handful for the experienced Bayern backline. In what had been an impressive season so far, the friendly was another addition to a growing collection of top-quality performances and if observing scouts wanted greater insight into the then-21-year-old, this display proved how good he was. Soon, Europe would take notice, with the likes of Liverpool and Borussia Dortmund interested – Jürgen Klopp, then of 'Die Borussen', even admitted his regret over not making a concrete move. Mané himself revealed later on that Guardiola was also set on bringing him to the Allianz Arena while the Spanish coach was there.

Six months after that display, Mané moved to the Premier League with Southampton, where Ronald Koeman was building a new team after the departures of several key figures. The winger would go on to achieve many successes in his career, doing well on the south coast for two years before moving to Liverpool in 2016, where he won the Champions League, claimed the African Player of the Year gong and finished fourth in the running for the Ballon d'Or – even earning a vote from Lionel Messi, the winner – all in 2019. However, it was at Salzburg that it all started for him and his success began a unique relationship between the Austrian giants and Africa that has seen several players and the club benefit. He is, arguably, Salzburg's best signing in the Red Bull era.

Signed from FC Metz, who were relegated from Ligue 2 in 2011/12, this was a statement of intent from Salzburg. The French club hadn't made the best of Mané's talents and the third tier in France was not where he was meant to be. Salzburg believed he fitted their renewed vision, led by Ralf Rangnick, and their scouts had been watching him for several months – starting all the way back at the 2012 summer Olympics in London. It wasn't until an intervention from Rangnick himself that a move was completed as he believed Mané's profile aligned perfectly with the club's philosophy.

Rangnick told *The Athletic*: 'I went to their League Cup game against Tours [in August 2012]. Sadio played very well, which worked a little against us that day. I remember meeting with Metz's president after the game. He insisted that they would only sell him for €4m. That was a huge fee for us, especially for a third-division player in France.' The risk was worth it as Mané would repay the faith by scoring 45 goals in 87 games as well as contributing to the league and cup double in his final season. He would leave for over five times the price and, in the midst of a culture change, Red Bull would start to see massive potential in the French and, primarily, African markets.

For the final two months before his departure, Mané shared the dressing room with Naby Keïta who, just like the Senegalese, had been signed from a relegated Ligue 2 club, in this case Istres. Gérard Houllier was a major influence in the club's transfer strategy in his role as Red Bull's global sports director. His knowledge of the French market and contacts opened up a number of doors and clear pathways were created for young footballers. Houllier was uncompromising on Keïta's talent. The Guinean impressed in Austria, moving to RB Leipzig just two years later where he was at his best again. Within a season, Liverpool agreed a massive €60m fee for his transfer ahead of the 2018/19 campaign, so it was another successful transaction for Red Bull.

The success of the two has seen Red Bull delve into the African markets even further. Although the two players were purchased from French clubs, it was in Africa where they were raised, and Red Bull began to go straight to the source. African players' athleticism combined with their intelligence suited the cluster's ethos perfectly while the economic benefit they brought was clear to see – they were easily affordable and provided a high sell-on value. Recent times have seen scouts working in countries like Mali, Ghana and the Ivory Coast. In Mali, Red Bull formed links with the JMG Academy, which has seen them acquire players like Amadou Haidara and Mohamed Camara. The academy, named after former French coach Jean-Marc Guillou (who gave Arsène Wenger his first break in coaching), has locations in countries like Algeria, Egypt, Madagascar and more. Additionally, there is Yeelen Olympique, one of the most popular academies in Mali.

Red Bull have also grown operations in Zambia, whose football approach changed drastically after they won the African Cup of Nations in 2012. Salzburg currently have two Zambian players in their first team: Patson Daka and Enock Mwepu. Both of them joined the Austrians in 2017 when they were still teenagers and were honed at Kafue Celtic, a famed Zambian club. Based in the country's capital of Lusaka and founded in 2002 (as Lusaka Celtic), they have always had a good youth system and some of Zambia's finest players, such as Stopilla Sunzu, Kennedy Mweene, Nathan Sinkala and Jackson Mwanza have come from there.

Also heavily involved in Red Bull's relationship with African teams and players is 12Managament, a consultancy service run by former Tottenham Hotspur and Sevilla player Frédéric Kanouté. The Malian has been working with young players in the region for several years and his agency even brokered the deal for Daka and Mwepu that saw them move to Austria.

Benjamin Siwale, a spokesperson for the Celtics, told me about what piqued Salzburg's interest when signing Daka and Mwepu: 'It was more hunger, determination and focus. One thing you'll find common with many African players is that they don't have the hunger to succeed. Most people just want to play football to be comfortable in life and not really make progress and that is why lots of Africans fail when they go to Europe. It's because they get there and they think they've made it to the big time. With Daka and Mwepu, every time Frédéric Kanouté was around in Zambia, he was watching games of theirs. He was seeing in their play and their life off the pitch, for them their life was always about football. That was a good sign – he knew these players would be good enough. The track record Kafue Celtic had also made it look good. They were very well prepared mentally.'

Kanouté's agency manages several African players, including two other Salzburg players, Sékou Koïta and Youba Diarra (both from Mali). Daka and Mwepu are the only two Zambians playing in Europe who are on his radar and he has started to pay keen attention to the growth in football in the country. His experiences and links certainly make him a resourceful person and Siwale believes he's a huge credit to African football: 'Kanouté took interest in the set-up and what he does is he flies in coaches just to train the players once in a while in order to make sure they have European training and I think that helps. I wouldn't say there's an agreement between us per se, but I would say that he is happy with the development that comes out of Kafue Celtic and he is all about developing players in Africa. In Zambia, he's more focused on just seeing the teams grow and obviously the way things are happening with Kafue Celtic and the buzz that's coming from around because of Daka and Mwepu is a big plus for us.'

Siwale adds: 'It's probably put us on the map for people to notice and anyone that looks into the past history will find out that Zambia's former captains and some of Zambia's greats have all come out of the Celtics. I would say that we are one of the most successful clubs in Zambia because of the quality of the players we've produced and how we've exported them. Additionally, we've been able to continue to find and develop talent here and there. At the moment, we have the likes of Francisco Mwepu, who is Enock's younger brother. He is currently on loan at Red Arrows. We have Alassane Diarra, who came in from Mali, he's also on loan at Red Arrows. Also, Tony Mundia, who is called the "Zambian Neymar" – there are players who are being monitored often.'

Mwepu had been one of Zambia's star performers at the 2017 U-20 World Cup in South Korea. This came just months after the country had won the U-20 African Cup of Nations. Nicknamed 'the Computer' for his intelligence and efficiency in midfield, he signed for Salzburg just two weeks after Zambia's campaign in the Far East ended, after they managed to reach the quarter-finals, losing to Italy. Mwepu scored twice in the tournament, first in the opener against Iran – a fine shot from the left wing to level the scores – and then against Germany in the round of 16 with a confident finish. For him, football was always a way of life and Mwepu kept his head down with one objective in mind.

'For them it's always been focus. Football first, family second for the both of them [Mwepu and Daka]. Mwepu comes from a devout Christian family so he's been very disciplined in the way he's been brought up. Every single day for him was always about training,' Siwale says. 'Fun fact about him: after he moved to Salzburg, he bought a car but when he was growing up, his older brother Emmanuel had been trying to teach him how to drive. He would always say, "I'm not going learn to drive until I buy my own car," and he did just that because of the success he's clearly achieved. That's a story he tells other footballers. He always says, "Guys, you can do it; you don't need anybody to tell you you can – it's all about you and how you make your life," and for him, he's made a name for himself.'

His compatriot Daka moved to Austria six months before him but has enjoyed a similar trajectory. They were together in the younger national teams and moved forward, giving Zambian football two identifiable figures. Daka, however, enjoyed more success at club level, being a part of the UEFA Youth League-winning squad in 2017 and even scoring the equaliser in the final against Benfica after coming on as a substitute. This is also where the importance of FC Liefering is shown. The farm club has been a home to several foreign talents who, like Daka, have been given the chance to grow and adapt to European football in a more controlled and less pressurised environment.

In the 2019/20 season, the forward was afforded more chances in the Salzburg first team under Jesse Marsch and he did well. After the sale of Erling Håland to Borussia Dortmund in January 2020, Daka was thrust into the spotlight with the goalscoring responsibility falling on his young shoulders. He showed no signs of pressure and took on the challenge, netting

27 goals across all competitions during the 2019/20 season, 24 of which came in the Bundesliga – the second most in the league. That record made him one of the most consistent forwards in Europe.

Siwale says: 'They've always been focused on training, on improving, on getting better, focused on trying to be the players that would put young Africans on the map. That's what they've been trying to do, and you can see it all happening. We learned that Daka, statistically speaking, was the best striker in Europe [at the time the COVID-19 pandemic halted football in March 2020]. An article compiled the stats of the top 11 leagues in Europe and according to it he was up there. There is talk about him moving to other clubs, but that story is for another day. Looking at those stats, it's showing you how hard Daka works – especially after the departure of Erling Håland.'

Salzburg's far-reaching scouting network has reaped its rewards in recent times, and they have one of the most diverse squads in Europe. In their Champions League clash against Liverpool at Anfield in September 2019, their starting XI consisted of four Austrians, two Zambians, and one each from Denmark, Cameroon, Hungary, Japan and South Korea. On the bench, there was one each from Ghana, Mali, Brazil, Switzerland, Norway, Japan and Austria. This consistency was carried throughout the season and it's something that is widely appreciated by niche footballing nations – especially those in Africa.

'I must praise Salzburg because usually you have problems with African players in Europe, but they find the best of the best, those that are hungry to succeed and those that are more determined to make a name for themselves,' says Siwale. 'Looking at African players, you usually get someone that is going to be gifted on either side of the pitch. For them, they're getting a powerhouse of a player so, as long as they get the best out of him as a youngster, they are definitely guaranteed a player worth developing.'

Siwale heaps further praise on the model in Salzburg, believing that their experiences and success on the big stage is of inspiration to many and provides a platform for emerging international youngsters: 'With Salzburg, they take younger players and they work with them before selling them by the age of 24 or 25, because football is a game where the younger you are, the easier it is to teach you. Salzburg are like another Ajax: using youth to achieve their goals and succeed locally as well as on the big stage, as we saw in the 2019/20 season when they played Chelsea and Real Madrid [in pre-season] and against Liverpool [in the Champions League], where they put up a fight at Anfield. That was good to see, and especially as they were all young players. Koïta, Daka and Mwepu are good examples – they [Salzburg] are really putting themselves out there, balancing between the youth and the slightly experienced names while focusing on the former and they have good coaches to support that, who are getting the most out of the players.'

In the short-run, the goal for both Daka and Mwepu is to make their mark in Salzburg and if they continue in the same vein, they are certain to become household names in the future for club and country. Siwale and Kafue Celtic have seen them go from boys to men to heroes in Austria and they have lofty ambitions for them. Zambian football has seen a few names come and make an impact in Europe, but the trajectory that is expected for their two stars of the modern day is sure to give the country a greater reputation and more attention in the near future.

Siwale says: 'Looking at how things have gone in the past, it's no secret that Liverpool monitor Red Bull's players a lot. Mwepu is a very big Liverpool fan so I would want to see him playing for Liverpool one day. It's something that he used to talk about. That's not in his hands – all he can do is try to play his best, which he has been doing. This season, he's been given more time in the team and he's made the most of his chances and I think the coach really likes him. For Daka, filling

Håland's boots is a big challenge but he's doing it well. He's rising to the occasion, getting his goals and he's recorded a good tally so far for a striker – especially for a young African striker who, as I said, often lack discipline. So, for his age, he is doing well, he obviously wants to play and reach certain heights and I see him doing that.'

Since 2012/13, Ragnick's first season, 19 African players have played under the Red Bull umbrella in Europe – that's either Salzburg, Leipzig or Liefering. Out of the 19, there have been five Malians, five Ghanaians, two Zambians, two Nigerians and one each from Senegal, Benin, Guinea, Cameroon and the Ivory Coast. Two have represented Leipzig in the Bundesliga. Recent years have seen increased scouting and more signings and, given their track record, it wouldn't come as a surprise to see Red Bull alumni achieving big things across Europe.

COMFORTABLE WITH
BEING UNCOMFORTABLE

AT HALF-TIME in the Champions League group stage match between Liverpool and Red Bull Salzburg at Anfield, Jesse Marsch gave an impassioned speech to rouse his team. The Austrian champions were 3-1 down to the blistering European champions and Marsch, speaking in English, German and universally understood expletives, asked his team for more. He wanted his players to play their natural game, to stick to their philosophy, to give respect to the competition they were playing in as well as the occasion, but not as much to the opposition. By the time they had visited Merseyside in early October 2019, Salzburg had already scored a mammoth 55 goals across all competitions in just 12 matches – an average of 4.58 goals per game. He wanted to see that again.

'How many fouls have we committed? Maybe two. It's not a fucking friendly! This is a Champions League game! We must physically compete on the field. Get fucking stuck in with a push. We've shown a lot of respect for the opposition when they play – a lot of respect! Are they good? Yeah, they are for sure. But we're playing all nice with weak pushes, not with any good tackles or fight! … We have already seen that they are good, but we can be better. We can put more life into it. Trust yourself, show physical strength, foul them. They aren't that dangerous with corners and advancing forward, we have more. That's our greatest strength right now,' said Marsch at half-time against Liverpool.

In the next 45 minutes, Salzburg levelled the scores but then lost 4-3; Mohamed Salah scored the winner some 20 minutes from time. The loss felt like a win in many ways. Coming back from a position like the one Salzburg found themselves in at the break hadn't been achieved by many against Liverpool in recent times, but this match earned the team plenty of plaudits. Despite being around for a decade, Salzburg – at least in their current form – had never played in the Champions League and the home of the reigning champions was the perfect place to make a mark. The praise wasn't just reserved for the players, it went to the manager as well – surely, everyone believed, he had weaved some magic at half-time? Marsch had been accustomed to fighting against the odds and sticking with what he believed in – he had been doing it for most of his managerial career, right from his early days in MLS.

The former midfielder played in MLS throughout his career and in 2012 was given the opportunity to become the first head coach of expansion franchise, Montreal Impact. Immediately, the American immersed himself in Quebec culture, learning French and displaying his command of the language in his press conferences. The city with the largest French-speaking population outside of Paris took a quick liking to their new young coach, who was just 38 at the time, and the fans were keen on seeing what he would do on the pitch.

As part of a wave of former MLS players who had been making the move into coaching at that time, Marsch had one important advantage over the rest, which was that he had worked with some of the best in American coaching, including Bob Bradley, his mentor. The pair first worked together when Marsch was a player at Princeton Tigers, the varsity team of Princeton University. Later on, the pair were together in MLS with DC United, Chicago Fire and Chivas USA. When

Bradley took up the job as the head coach of the United States men's national team, he appointed Marsch as his assistant. The experience was invaluable, the respect between the pair is strong and Marsch took what he had learned to Canada.

With a relatively aged squad and a manager getting his first taste of a senior role in coaching, there wasn't much expected of the Impact. After a slow start to the 2012 season, they finished 12th – a respectable return in their debut season. However, Joey Sapputo, the franchise's trigger-happy owner, didn't see it that way. In November 2012, after just one season of leading the team, Marsch left, citing differences in coaching philosophies and the direction they wanted to take the team in. While the stint was largely seen as a failure, this had been a good place for Marsch to show his footballing acumen. It was where he learned what players needed not just in a coach, but in a leader as well, and it was a crucial experience for him.

After leaving Montreal, Marsch, his wife and three home-schooled kids embarked on a five-month tour around 29 different countries. Having started off in Hong Kong, they went across south-east Asia, hopping on and off trains, buses and boats as they made their way east towards Europe. Marsch developed a term, 'transfer time', to describe the adjustment period the family needed when they arrived in each location. Each time they would get off a plane or a train to find their new destination, their transfer time would decrease. The sabbatical also had hints of soccer, as he visited former coaches in the United Arab Emirates and Egypt, former team-mates in the Czech Republic and Belgium and friends in various other cities. Overall, this was an enriching experience and elements of the trip were essential in the building of his coaching career.

The Wisconsin native then returned to his alma mater, Princeton University, to assist former head coach Jim Barlow. The ultimate ambition, though, was to return to MLS and continue coaching at the highest level in America.

That opportunity would come out of the blue in 2015, when, in a controversial move, Marsch was appointed as the head coach of the New York Red Bulls. The move didn't go down well with the fans, who didn't consider him an attractive prospect at all. He was replacing Mike Petke, a fan-favourite and beloved figure in the Big Apple for his career that had seen him represent the Red Bulls as a player and a coach. His sacking caused uproar, seeing as he was their most successful coach and the only one to bring them any silverware. The fact that he was being replaced by a relative rookie in management didn't help matters either.

To calm emotions, the club held a 'town hall' meeting (featuring sporting director Ali Curtis, general manager Marc de Grandpre, goalkeeper Luis Robles and new head coach Marsch) with its season ticket holders, but that didn't go as planned. One fan angrily asked: 'Why did you fire Petke? No more bullshit. No more corporate lingo,' to which Marsch defiantly replied: 'You don't have to like me, and you may never like me. That is the role of the coach. That isn't important to me. What's important to me is the team … If we lose, you will hate me. If we win, maybe you will put up with me. But give this team a chance to take the field and compete.' Soon, he was asked about what his style of play would be, to which he responded: 'To get quickly and briefly into the playing style, this is an energy drink … a more dynamic and up-tempo game.' This infuriated supporters even further. For long-term fans, Red Bull's ownership could hardly be tolerated and referencing the company when asked about football put Marsch on the back foot early on.

The initial weeks were almost farcical and Marsch was seen as the owners' 'yes man' – someone who would adequately follow orders and help tighten the purse strings. However, he was intent on proving he was more than what many believed. His attention to detail and diligent planning showed in the early weeks of the season. The Red Bulls usually set up in a 4-2-3-1, with a heavy emphasis on coordinated pressing. While he was at Princeton University, he had often observed how the rowing teams operated, how they pushed in sync to get past the finish line and achieve a common goal. Marsch applied those ideas to football as well: if a team did not press together and work non-stop, then they would fall apart. Hints of this were seen in Montreal, but they truly shone in New York.

Marsch developed an attractive brand of football based around his ideas of high pressing and compactness without the ball as well as vertical orientation and speed with it. Against all expectations, the Red Bulls grew to become one of the most dominant teams in the league in the 2015 season as they picked up some mightily impressive results: a 4-1 win over the New England Revolution, a 3-0 win over DC United, 2-1 wins over Columbus Crew and Montreal Impact and a double over New York City FC, the new MLS franchise and their domestic rivals. Despite that, the MLS Cup didn't arrive as they fell to the Crew in the Eastern Conference Final. However, the Supporters' Shield proved their quality. By the end, everyone sang Marsch's praises. With the lowest payroll in the league and a fresh system for the players, it could be said that the Red Bulls had overachieved. A club record of 18 wins and 60 points also earned Marsch the MLS Coach of the Year gong; the gaffes at the start of the season were forgotten.

The effect of the lack of investment in the team showed at the start of 2016. After selling Matt Miazga, their best centre-half, to Chelsea and not making any significant signings, the Red Bulls had a slow start to the season but eventually picked up. Players like Bradley Wright-Phillips and Sacha Kljestan would enjoy an upturn in form while they even thumped New York City FC 7-0. However, this felt like a lost season as their shortcomings in the MLS Cup play-offs continued. The Red Bulls were good but couldn't hit the heights of greatness.

It was at this point that Marsch started building on his ambitions to work in Europe and he would become a hugely important example for other American coaches. While American players had gained acceptance across the Atlantic, it was rare to see coaches replicating that feat. Bradley's underwhelming stints – especially in the Premier League with Swansea City in 2017/18 – didn't help the situation, no matter how well he may have done elsewhere, but Marsch was adamant about changing the status quo. In March 2017, he missed a few days of the Red Bulls' training to go to Scotland and work on his UEFA Pro Licence in order to boost his prospects.

Amidst all of that, the 2017 season was very similar to the previous year. Little investment, decent results but a few tactical tweaks to show Marsch's adaptability. He often switched to a three-man backline with two wing-backs, giving more responsibility to the experienced Daniel Royer and more time to Tyler Adams, who he wanted to integrate into the first team with a view towards shaping the team around him in the future. That season, once again, would not bring much joy but the following year was historic. Although it started with some inconsistency, their form picked up and the Red Bulls went on a rampage in front of goal, picking up some big wins. Midway through the season, however, Marsch left with the best record for a coach in the club's history (76 wins, 30 draws and 45 losses) and he wasn't there to see the team win the Supporters' Shield at the end of 2018.

After Ralph Hasenhüttl's departure from RB Leipzig at the end of the 2017/18 season and with Julian Nagelsmann's arrival scheduled for exactly a year later, Ralf Rangnick stepped back into the dugout to take charge of 'Die Rotten Bullen' for the second time in his career. He would appoint Marsch as his assistant in what was set to be a two-year deal. This was the experience the American wanted in Europe and he even rejected the opportunity to become the head coach of the United States men's national team after their failure to qualify for the World Cup in Russia. Leaving a top job to be an assistant in Europe may have been seen as a backwards move by some, but it was here that Marsch would get his first taste of European football. Rangnick said: 'I know the league, the team, and I speak the language. That isn't the case yet for Jesse Marsch, so that's why he will be working as an assistant coach.'

Leipzig would enjoy a decent season, reaching the DFB Pokal Final and finishing third in the Bundesliga. Marsch would even help out behind the scenes, setting up the team's disciplinary 'punishments' – as noted previously. In April 2019, however, Marsch would take a huge leap. Following Marco Rose's decision to move to Borussia Mönchengladbach for the next campaign, Red Bull decided to promote from within and give Marsch the top job in Austria for the next season. This was an indication that he had done things right over the years and showed Red Bull's faith in him.

Just like in New York, Marsch wasn't a welcomed figure in Salzburg. When his appointment was announced, the Salzburg fans hung a banner in the stadium during the match against Sturm Graz which read *'Nein zu Marsch'* – no to Marsch. However, any doubts over his abilities were quickly put away in his early months at the club. He immediately adapted to the culture; having learned German during his time in Leipzig, he tried to perfect it as much as possible when in Austria and his first press conference was done in the language. On the pitch, the start was emphatic and in a matter of weeks, everyone was on board.

Under Marsch, Salzburg deployed a 4-2-2-2 and they were an exquisite attacking force as the two players in the heart of midfield sufficiently supported the two wide players, who would often join in with the two forwards. The attacking play – often resembling the successful style of Rose – featured quick transitions from back to front with flexible interplay setting up chances for the front four. From a defensive standpoint, the pressing was a bit different from Marsch's predecessor. The wide midfielders would join the centre-forwards in pressing the opposing backline which created four-on-four situations and led to possession turnovers. When defending deeper, the wide midfielders would provide cover for the full-backs and create a superiority in numbers. This was widely evident – and often successful – across the league as well as in the Champions League.

Marsch was uncompromising about giving young players a chance, making them confident and using their fearlessness as well as lack of experience as a positive. Takumi Minamino was the lynchpin in this side, having been used sporadically before. The Japanese was the hub of distribution, creating attacking opportunities at will and his movement stood out. Maximilian Wöber, Masaya Okugawa and Dominik Szoboszlai were other names whose confidence grew over the course of the season and they became better footballers. The mental growth of the players propelled them to do well and they picked up some incredible results such as an Erling Håland-inspired 6-2 win over Genk in the Champions League, a 2-1 away success over Rapid Wien in the Austrian Cup which featured a late winner and then overcoming LASK in the semi-finals of the same competition.

The second half of the season saw a slump, however. Losing Minamino and Håland was detrimental to the team. Having lost out in a tough Champions League group featuring Liverpool, Napoli and Genk, Marsch's team were also knocked out of the Europa League by Eintracht Frankfurt – a side led by another of Salzburg's former coaches, Adi Hütter. At the time of the COVID-19 outbreak which halted football across Europe in spring 2020, they were six points behind LASK in the race for the Bundesliga. LASK, a team that nearly went bankrupt in 2013 and was playing in the third division as recently as 2014, have been troublesome. They beat Salzburg at home in the league in February 2020 – a rare feat for a visiting side – and caused a few upsets in Austria.

Salzburg had a bit of luck after LASK were deducted points for breaching lockdown rules during the enforced coronavirus break, which meant Marsch's team were back on top. In their championship group for the Austrian league title they were unstoppable, proving just why they deserved to be champions. Patson Daka had a season to remember after coming in for the departed Håland. His breakthrough campaign saw him net 27 goals across all competitions and put him on the radar as another top talent coming through the Salzburg ranks. Overall, Salzburg ended the season with 110 league goals – a joint league record with Roger Schmidt's 2014 team (who scored the same number of goals with four more games).

Marsch also continued Salzburg's dominance in the cup, as they steamrolled past teams on their way to a seventh league and cup double. Twenty-three goals were scored across their five knockout matches, which included a semi-final success over LASK. Second-division Austria Lustenau were beaten 5-0 in the final as Salzburg extended their reputation as Austria's premier club.

The American coach's start, despite a few bumpy moments, had been impressive. Rumours linked him with a move to Borussia Dortmund, something the Germans denied later on, but a move to the Bundesliga is almost inevitable: three of Salzburg's last five coaches found their feet there and Marsch certainly fits the bill. He will need more experience and success in Austria, though, but the talent is clearly there.

Wherever he goes, he tends to win over supporters against all expectations. Marsch is always on the hunt for a challenge and is willing to take a chance in unfamiliar territory; something which gives him a thrill. In his own words he has 'gotten more comfortable with being uncomfortable.' How his career shapes up from here will be interesting to see: will he succeed at Salzburg like all the managers before him – perhaps take them a step further and do well in the Champions League? Will Red Bull continue to have faith in him and strive to keep him under their umbrella – maybe move him back to the German Bundesliga with Leipzig, this time in the hot seat, when Nagelsmann is done? When will his certain move into the head coach role of the United States men's national team occur? Marsch is still young, but his potential is immense.

NEW YORK'S FINEST

EARLY IN a game against DC United in July 2018, Bradley Wright-Phillips' shot squirmed under goalkeeper David Ousted in an immense moment for player, club and league. This wasn't the prettiest of goals, but it was hugely significant. As Wright-Phillips wheeled away in jubilant celebration, he took off his red away Red Bulls' shirt that boasted his number 99 and revealed the white home shirt with the number 100. The Lewisham-born forward had just hit a century of MLSgoals in record time and his name was set to enter the soccer history books.

For much of Wright-Phillips' career, he has been fighting against expectations that were first set by his father Ian Wright, whose legendary career saw him become Arsenal's greatest goal-scorer, and then by his older brother Shaun, who enjoyed stints at Manchester City and Chelsea. Bradley's career hadn't quite hit the same heights, as he had underwhelming spells across the English league ladder with Manchester City, Southampton, Plymouth Argyle, Charlton Athletic and Brentford. With his love for the game drained and eyes set on a new challenge, Wright-Phillips found an unlikely home in New York.

'I wanted a change. I was playing for Charlton Athletic at the time and in my last season I went out on loan [to Brentford]. Then I had a few more offers to stay in England but I just didn't want to do the same thing – I didn't want to play in League One or the Championship,' Wright-Phillips tells me. 'I wasn't enjoying my football at the time and my agent came to me with an offer from the New York Red Bulls, having already had a player there, and he said the club wanted to see me train. I thought, "I'll go there" – I wasn't thinking of signing – I just thought, "I'll go and see how they're doing things, how their training facility is, how the team is like, how they're playing and so on." But, as soon as I got there, I realised it was all going very well, and I wanted to stay and continue.

'At the time I got there [2013], there were players like Thierry Henry, Tim Cahill and Peguy Luyindula – they had some good players there. There was also Lloyd Sam, a friend of mine who I had known from before. So, it was very easy for me to settle in there. I liked the team and I had always wanted to play with someone like Henry because I'm a big Arsenal fan, so once I got there, it was a no-brainer.'

Playing in New York where athletes are always under a spotlight – even if soccer isn't the USA's most fancied sport – there wasn't much expected from Wright-Phillips. The New York Red Bulls won the Supporters' Shield in 2013, but Wright-Phillips' involvement was limited, having been hindered by injuries. The Red Bulls considered releasing him from their roster at the end of that season, but it was an intervention from their global head of football Gérard Houllier that prevented it from happening. He believed Wright-Phillips deserved another chance to prove his worth and that was enough motivation for the Englishman to go on and excel in the Big Apple. The forward would take the opportunity granted to him with both hands.

MLS' reputation may not be too high compared to some of the most popular leagues in Europe, but there were several challenges faced by players off the pitch which take plenty of time to adapt to. Some key differences between American and European football affect a player's fitness, drive and continuity and, for Wright-Phillips, it took a while to acclimatise.

He says: 'When I first got there, it wasn't how Red Bull do things now. We were different – there was a lot more talent in the team, but we didn't have the system or the way of playing. It was more like if the big players could make big plays [we would do well]. That was how it was in 2013 and 2014. Our style of football was up to the mark, we were one of the better teams in the league and we should've won a cup. The main difference I felt was the travelling – that was tough. Also, the weather, that was the hardest thing for me to adjust to. Everything else football-wise was just about the same, but the travelling and the weather were the hardest things.'

Unlike other leagues in America such as the NBA, MLB or NHL (National Hockey League), MLS rules state that teams can only use charter flights for four travel legs – not even four games – which means players mostly have to travel by commercial flights, which may include long-haul stopovers or extended journeys as they go across the USA and sometimes Canada. In a lengthy season (in 2020 the league has 26 teams and is due to increase to 30 by 2022), charter flights are effectively used for just two league matches so travelling can prove to be an exhausting process. Extraordinary circumstances such as cancelled flights, extreme weather or a lack of suitable options are accounted for; however, the fatigue still affects teams.

Despite the hassle, the 2014 season saw a revival in Wright-Phillips' form. This was one of the most consistent seasons by an individual in MLS history as the forward netted an extraordinary 27 goals in 32 appearances – the highest in the league that season.

Despite the record, the Red Bulls failed to bring home a trophy as they lost the conference final against the New England Revolution having finished fourth in the Eastern Conference. However, Wright-Phillips did form an exceptional partnership with Thierry Henry.

'I remember speaking to a few of the players when I got there. I won't lie, I was very ignorant about the league and I thought, "I'll play the 2013 season and I'm going back." I remember I couldn't get into the team because I had two hamstring injuries and it was tough,' says Wright-Phillips. 'Then I spoke to Henry. He was telling me what to do – a load of little things to improve on – and I remember working together with him in the beginning of 2014 and he wanted to assist me. He wasn't just a striker, he was an all-round player. He told me that whenever he got the ball, I should make little smart runs and he'd try and find me. So, early in pre-season in 2014, I worked on my movement, worked on hitting the target, finding the corners and in the games it just came naturally. I knew I had someone who could give me the ball in dangerous areas and that worked out very well.'

An Arsenal man through and through, it comes as no surprise that Henry is Wright-Phillips' footballing idol. At that stage in his career, he cites the Frenchman's influence as a vital aspect of his rejuvenation across the Atlantic. Having signed at the age of 28, the late resurgence in Wright-Phillips' career was largely helped by Henry's support off the pitch and creativity, calm and experience on it – something the English forward cherished in the short time they spent together at the club. Wright-Phillips says: 'For me, that was amazing. I learned so much sharing the pitch and the dressing room with him and playing games together. Getting some knowledge and talking to him every day was a big lesson for me. Obviously, the way my career was going, playing with Henry was not something that would've happened, would it? It was really nice for me, it helped me a lot and it revitalised my career. Every day was good, we got quite close – there was no particular moment that stands out for me.'

Following Henry's retirement ahead of the 2015 season, as well as a change in management with Jesse Marsch replacing Mike Petke, there were doubts over whether

Wright-Phillips could continue his superb form. Henry was a leader in the dressing room and an instrumental creator on the pitch; losing him meant losing a key source of the Red Bulls' attacking prowess. Marsch's relative inexperience in senior management also raised fears and many believed the progress made by the club would be derailed as a result of these two major changes.

However, those worries were put to the side when the league kicked off once again as the Red Bulls would go on to win another Supporters' Shield. Marsch's impressive pressing style earned plaudits from across the country and Wright-Phillips discovered new elements to his game: he scored 17 goals that season and even set up seven more – an increase of five from the previous year. In the middle of the campaign, his brother Shaun joined him in New York and this time the roles were reversed – it was the older brother who had to play catch-up rather than the other way around, which had been the case for much of their careers. In their first game together, against the Philadelphia Union, the older set up the younger for the opener in a 3-1 success.

Petke and Marsch were two different coaches with two different styles. The former focused on the players' strengths and giving them all the freedom while the latter was more meticulous on collective organisation. Both are widely admired in New York and Wright-Phillips most certainly enjoyed working with and learning from the pair.

Wright-Phillips: 'I was with Petke first. He didn't base too much around his own philosophy, the best thing he had was the players' trust. He could relax. Petke didn't do much with regards to team-talks, it was just about how we played. When I did play under him, I felt like I didn't have too much pressure on me because there wasn't a way of playing per se: I just had to go out and score goals. I don't think he was the biggest tactician, but I did feel free, I felt like I could go out there and play my natural game.'

He continues: 'With Marsch, I think, without being disrespectful to anybody else, he was the best I had out of the three coaches at New York Red Bulls and his career has gone on to show that. He was different, he had a way of playing and he demanded a lot from the players. Every player improved under him because he didn't allow players to get distracted. Training was hard; there was a specific way of playing and if you didn't do that then you wouldn't play. His man-management was also very good. He'd often have one-on-ones with the players, treat us well and develop different strategies to deal with each player. He was excellent and that was when we were really a force to be reckoned with. Before him, we probably had a lot more talent, but we also weren't that great. After Marsch arrived, we were a proper team as he steered us in the right direction, and it was enjoyable.'

Marsch's positive start in Europe also doesn't shock Wright-Phillips; in his mind, this was expected, given the American coach's astuteness: 'Wherever he goes, he's a confident man. He believes in what he's doing, what he's saying, his tactics and how things should be done. Once he goes somewhere else, he will be the same and if you don't want to work, if you don't want to be the best, he won't have the time for you, and to see what he's doing in Austria doesn't surprise me at all.'

Henry's departure didn't stop Wright-Phillips from breaking more records. In 2016, he netted 24 league goals, becoming the first player in MLS history to score over 20 in two different seasons. Additionally, his tally of 68 goals between 2014 and 2016 was the biggest across a three-year spell by any MLS player, breaking the record held by Chris Wondolowski (62 between 2010 and 2012). It was in that season that he took the honour of being the club's highest goalscorer and he ran with it. Once again that season, Wright-Phillips claimed the Golden Boot, holding off David Villa by one.

It was in this period that Wright-Phillips would form a fine partnership with American midfielder Sacha Kljestan, who had taken up the mantle as the team's creator in chief. This was a fine duo that combined frequently for the Red Bulls' goals as Kljestan's 20 assists in a single season were the second-highest in league history, only behind the iconic Carlos Valderrama, who created 27 in 2000. This was a relationship that Wright-Phillips relished: 'He was another one that was really clever in the final third and he has a decent understanding of the game in general. We formed a nice little partnership where, again, I was just playing my natural game and he adapted to me and my style. He always happened to find me in dangerous areas. He got the club assists record as well and was a good player to play with.'

Wright-Phillips and Kljestan's partnership continued in 2017 with the forward adding 17 to his goals tally while the midfielder had the same number of assists. The MLS Cup continued to elude them, however, as they fell short to Toronto FC, the eventual champions. To add further salt to the wounds, the Red Bulls also lost to Sporting Kansas City in the US Open Cup Final.

The next year, 2018, saw some seismic changes as well as the emergence of Tyler Adams, who was one of the best defensive midfielders in the league at the age of 19, while other academy names, such as Sean Davis, had prominent roles in the first team. Wright-Phillips believes the academy was a crucial aspect of the Red Bulls' machine and praises the club's willingness to give youngsters a chance:

'The academy is a big deal for them – like it should be – and the New York Red Bulls academy is really good. The players that come through play a lot of first-team games and there are a couple of players that have got a big move,' he says. 'That's an example that they're not afraid to give young players a shot, they're not afraid to bring them to the first team early and they're not afraid to let them train with the big players. Even for pre-season, they'll bring a young academy team out for a few days and let them come around with us.

The Red Bulls are intent on making all the players at the club one team. It helps us all – they are truly passionate about growing the academy.'

The Red Bulls were far more impressive in 2018 and added yet another Supporters' Shield – the third in Wright-Phillips' time at the club. More goals followed for the forward, including his aforementioned 100th against DC United. By the end, the Red Bulls had set the MLS record for most points (71) and wins (22) in a single season, but the MLS Cup was still far away as they lost to Atlanta United in the Eastern Conference Final, once again a side that went all the way.

Midway through the campaign, Marsch decided to pursue his ambitions in Europe and it was Chris Armas, his assistant, who took over.

The two worked together for a short period of time before Wright-Phillips departed the club at the end of the 2019 campaign, during which he was troubled with injury issues. However, Wright-Phillips is appreciative of Armas' work and says his future could well have been in New York: 'Armas was another one who carried the Red Bull style. He wanted a bit more from us on the pitch, a bit more passing. He just did one or two things differently from Marsch and he was quite laid-back as well, but did stamp his authority when he had to. I didn't have a lot of time with Armas, it was about a year and a half.'

He adds: 'It wasn't necessarily me that made the decision to leave. In my mind, I've always said that if I could have, I would have stayed in New York and called time on my career there. But I think that the way Red Bull do things, I was a bit older and they look for younger options and I don't hate that. I only wish I had known a little earlier in that season, but it wasn't me that decided to leave.

'At the end it was decided that this was not the direction they wanted to go in anymore.'

BRADLEY WRIGHT-PHILLIPS NEW YORK RED BULLS RECORD	
SEASON	GOALS (ALL COMPETITIONS)
2013	2
2014	31 (won the MLS Golden Boot)
2015	18
2016	25 (won the MLS Golden Boot)
2017	24
2018	24
2019	2
TOTAL	126

At a club that hosted the likes of Lothar Matthäus, Youri Djorkaeff, Juan Pablo Ángel and Henry, amongst others, Wright-Phillips was the unlikely hero of the New York Red Bulls and MLS. Having ended his stint with an amazing record of 126 goals in 240 appearances across all competitions, he is undoubtedly their greatest goalscorer and arguably their greatest player ever, leaving the club's fans with some excellent memories. His famous number 99 was retired as a tribute to his achievements with the club and he is beloved by the Red Bulls' faithful. Wright-Phillips himself has some cherished memories of his time there.

He says: 'I have a lot of fine memories. Winning the Supporters' Shields were amazing and, coming from Europe, that's like winning the league. Obviously in MLS, you have to win the play-offs, but it was a big deal for us, nonetheless. The Golden Boot twice was great. We also had a game against New York City FC where we won that 7-0. There are a lot of good memories so it's difficult to pick one that stands out for me.'

Now playing across the coast at Los Angeles FC, the Englishman is optimistic of a bright future for himself and his former employers: 'For myself, I'm glad to get away from my injuries and I feel strong and fit. Everyone thinks I'm done but not many people know the back story – they think it's over. So, I'm looking forward to proving a lot of people wrong and I want to win the MLS Cup with LAFC – I feel we're in a strong position to do that. For the New York Red Bulls, I think they're going in the right direction. They've got a lot of good young players. They are a strong team to play against and I think they'll continue to do well. I've still got a lot of friends there, so I wish them the best and I'll keep an eye out for them.'

MADE IN STALYBRIDGE

IN THE summer of 2014, there was arguably no club in Europe that had a more impressive transfer window than Southampton. Having lost some of their top players from the previous season, including Luke Shaw, Adam Lallana and Dejan Lovren – players that featured in that year's World Cup in Brazil – things didn't look so good for the Saints.

However, their aggressive and intelligent transfer approach saw them replace these important names with some potent players from leagues across Europe: defender Toby Alderweireld came in on loan from Spain's Atlético Madrid; Graziano Pellè and Dušan Tadić joined from Dutch Eredivisie sides Feyenoord and Twente respectively; and most significantly, Sadio Mané swapped Austria's Red Bull Salzburg for the south coast of England.

Having also lost manager Mauricio Pochettino to Spurs, there weren't any massive expectations from the Ronald Koeman-led Southampton. By the end of the 2014/15 campaign, however, they had one of the stories of the season. A £25m profit on transfers, a seventh-place finish in the league, having been in the top four halfway through the campaign, and plaudits from the world over proved that Southampton were a smart, sustainable club. But while the praise was largely reserved for the players and the manager, there was one man in charge of making the tough decisions whose work went under the radar: Paul Mitchell.

About four years on from that glorious summer, Mitchell found himself at RB Leipzig. So, why did the Englishman from Stalybridge, Manchester, get appointed at one of the most quickly emerging clubs in the German Bundesliga – a rare move by a club in that league? A part of the answer can be found by looking into the work that Mitchell has been a part of.

Mitchell, a player who could play in defence and in midfield during his days on the pitch, saw his own career come to an end at the young age of 27 after recurring injury issues while at Milton Keynes Dons. He immediately joined the club's rejuvenated recruitment department, having initially carried out some tasks as an ambassador. When he worked alongside manager Karl Robinson, the Dons recognised his aptitude in talent identification and soon gave him massive responsibilities. The former Wigan Athletic player did a fine job with the League One club, enhancing their attention towards youth and streamlining their transfer activity by bringing them players to help them at the level they were at. In two seasons, MK Dons managed to make the play-offs, but didn't get promoted.

His efforts hadn't gone unnoticed and in 2012 he made a move to Championship side Southampton, a club that took pride in their philosophies and commitment towards developing their own. Mitchell was seen as the ideal fit for the Saints in this regard. Recent times had seen academy graduates make big moves – Gareth Bale to Tottenham, and Theo Walcott and Alex Oxlade-Chamberlain to Arsenal. All three enjoyed a decent level of success throughout their careers and Mitchell's job was to enrich the club's reputation for developing top-class players.

Working with sporting director Les Reed, the Manchester native's ability to analyse players was served by the club's incredible facilities – at the time, the Saints' football development centre had ten computer screens with matches watched throughout the day by full-time staff. In another department were a group of scouts who physically went out and hunted for talented players who might be as young as five years old – this group included Rod Ruddick, the man who had found Bale at the age of eight. Most interestingly, there was another small room fitted with a giant screen which was the most important sector in this centre. Labelled the 'black box', Southampton's self-designed computer software enabled Mitchell and his staff to watch any player, team or potential target of theirs anywhere in the world. A vital aspect of Mitchell's role was not just to arrange transfers but work out how players might fit in – and that's not just players that might potentially join in the future, but also the existing players at the club. All characteristics combined, it was a facility the Englishman has praised and made full use of.

Mitchell told the *Daily Telegraph*: 'Unless people have got a real black box underground, I've never heard of a training facility having something like that – having something designed and bespoke with that ability to deliver. It's not just recruitment. That's where the theory started, but I've seen the power of that room; to sit with Fraser Forster [former Southampton goalkeeper] when Dave Watson [the goalkeeping coach] is going through the pre- and the post-match with him or to even deliver to a young player we potentially want to sign into the academy and have him sit there with mum and dad and go through a visual presentation to say why he should choose Southampton; it's just a very powerful platform.' This level of attention to detail has made Southampton such a prominent club in player growth.

Within six months of Mitchell joining the Saints, they were promoted to the Premier League. In the transfer market, the club made some valuable additions, roping in the likes of Nathaniel Clyne, Maya Yoshida, Jay Rodriguez and Paulo

Gazzaniga. The results on the pitch, however, put them under pressure. The start was bad as Southampton won just one of their first ten games, with fans believing survival was unlikely. A few draws and sporadic wins then gave them control, but after manager Nigel Adkins was unexpectedly sacked in January 2013, there was confusion. In came Pochettino, whose command of English and prior managerial career wasn't the most appealing, but Mitchell and Reed had faith in their man. Southampton survived, finishing 14th, and then built a team capable of bettering that. When appointing the Argentine manager, Southampton had been aware of his famed 4-2-3-1 that had worked wonders at Espanyol. That summer, they made two notable signings to fit that system: Victor Wanyama and Lovren.

The results translated to the pitch as the Saints finished eighth in 2013/14 – their best standing in the top flight in over a decade – and that meant Mitchell and his decisions were vindicated. Pochettino immediately became the most sought-after manager in England and he would ring in the start of a fire sale by moving to Tottenham. The previously mentioned refurbishment of the squad commenced and, despite losing salient first-team names, they would end the transfer window better than they started.

However, despite setting the team up for success, Mitchell wasn't around to see Southampton doing well. He would join Pochettino in north London in late November as Spurs looked to this youthful partnership to establish the club as a Champions League regular. A year prior, the Lilywhites had essentially wasted the £85m that had been earned by the sale of Bale to Real Madrid on players that didn't fit the squad well. Now, they looked to rectify those errors. Mitchell's first signing was Dele Alli from his former club MK Dons, perhaps the most economical £5m spent by a top-flight club in recent times. That was followed by a summer that included a permanent move for Alderweireld, who had got his opening in the Premier League under Mitchell a year prior, and the Belgian defender was joined by Son Heung-min and Kieran Trippier.

With these new players to add to the pre-existing talented core of Hugo Lloris, Jan Vertonghen, Christian Eriksen and Harry Kane, Spurs would go on to become one of the most entertaining teams in Europe. Twice, they went close to winning the league title, in 2016 and 2017. They didn't win a trophy in the end, but there was still loads of pride to be taken from that period: the fact that they had they had the youngest team in the Premier League proved the quality of Mitchell and Pochettino's work at White Hart Lane.

Once again, Mitchell would not complete the ride. In August 2016, he asked to leave Spurs, with reports of a rift between him and chairman Daniel Levy, a tough negotiator who has proven difficult to deal with in the past. He was made to serve a 16-month notice period and even helped the club in the 2017 winter transfer window as Spurs looked to find an adequate replacement for their departing head of recruitment. There were whispers that Mitchell would move into management, but that didn't happen. Instead, he made an unlikely move to Germany in February 2018, where RB Leipzig were keen on acquiring his talents.

From Leipzig's point of view, they had just endured a disappointing winter transfer window during which they completed no permanent transfers and Ralf Rangnick believed Mitchell would help find the right attributes in their future dealings. In his presentation to the German media, Rangnick claimed that he was acquiring 'one of the most well-known and competent scouts in England' and that he 'will have a key role to play at the club'. He added that the Englishman was a touted figure and praised his career: 'Mitchell had offers from many clubs, having basically led Southampton back to the Premier League with players that he discovered and developed there. He then moved with [Mauricio] Pochettino to Tottenham, and for two years he played a massive part in improving the quality of their squad – predominately playing with by far the highest number of young players in a top Premier League team.'

Leipzig believed Mitchell fitted the bill and could work well within the club's intricate and successful transfer strategies. The reasons behind specifically choosing Mitchell aren't publicly known, but looking back, one can understand why he was given the reins as their head of recruitment and development. Firstly, he and Rangnick crossed paths when discussing Mané's transfer to Southampton in 2014. The German was in awe of the competence shown by the young Englishman and his eye for recognising and developing talent was most certainly pleasing. Mané's career taking off definitely worked in Mitchell's favour, but his own stints with Southampton and then Tottenham were clearly very good. He would prove to be a valuable addition to the RB Leipzig juggernaut, which prided itself upon its elite recruitment.

Secondly, it seemed ideal to have a successful, well-connected Brit working with them during a time when a wave of British talent had joined the German Bundesliga, with more expected to come. Mitchell's close links back home would come in handy for a club always on the hunt for the finest young names. In the year prior to his arrival, English youth had dominated international football: the U-21s reached the semi-finals of the European Championships, the U-20s won the World Cup, the U-19s won the Euros, the U-18s were heavily involved in winning the Toulon Tournament and the U-17s won the World Cup whilst also finishing as runners-up in the Euros. Surely, there were more exciting names in these squads, and it made perfect sense for Leipzig to have a man who knew the market so well on their side. Bundesliga clubs were keen on signing British talent after seeing the heights Borussia Dortmund would reach with Jadon Sancho. Leipzig themselves had trodden these waters in the past with deals for Oliver Burke in 2016 and Ademola Lookman on loan in 2018.

Finally, Mitchell's own positive track record and international reach was excellent. Previous years had seen him sign talents with great potential from Austria, Germany, France, Spain and more nations across Europe, whilst mostly staying within a tight budget. The average age of his 30 permanent signings for Spurs and Southampton was just 23.8 years old. He fitted in with Leipzig's philosophies in the transfer market: both wanted hungry, competent and economically sensible players for the club. In Mitchell, Red Bull had the perfect man.

In the Englishman's own words, refreshing a squad is pivotal for success and it is something he strives to keep doing wherever he goes. Speaking to *The Athletic*, he said: 'My philosophy is that you need, year-on-year, new voices, new profiles, just to stimulate the group. Just to keep the group competitive, to keep the group's daily training at its maximum – that competitive stimulation that all great teams have. It doesn't have to be a whole wave of new players. Two to three to four players every window, of the highest quality, that can try to break into that starting 11. It's crucial to continue being competitive at the very, very top echelons of the game. Any team, irrespective of natural age, needs refreshing and succession planning just to instigate the competitive element within the squad.'

Over the next two seasons, Mitchell and Leipzig would continue their far-reaching policy, signing the likes of Nordi Mukiele Matheus Cunha, Christopher Nkunku and Dani Olmo. So impressive was his work that he was heavily linked with a move back home to Manchester United, who were looking to end their own woes in the transfer market by bringing in a director of football to oversee their activity. However, Red Bull were intent on keeping their man and promoted him to work with Rangnick in 2019, keeping tabs on the cluster's international operations in New York and Brazil, with a view to opening pathways to their two European clubs in Salzburg and Leipzig. Doing well in the Americas is of paramount importance to the group as they recognise the talent in these parts and don't want to miss out on the potential.

Another crucial reason to keep him on board was to have him work with Julian Nagelsmann – the brightest prospect in German coaching. Red Bull saw this pairing being very similar to that of Mitchell and Pochettino: two young football minds who had excelled from a youthful age, with identical football ideologies and commitment to helping players reach their maximum level. With that in mind, Mitchell's focus towards the English market was also evident. In two summers, Leipzig completed loan moves for Arsenal's Emile Smith-Rowe and Ethan Ampadu from Chelsea whilst also re-signing Lookman from Everton in the summer of 2019, this time on a permanent basis. There is no doubt that given the talent in England and the fact that young players themselves have seen the benefits of moving to the Bundesliga, this relationship will only continue to grow.

Mitchell: 'I think our objective as a growing organisation is always to compete for top four now. We always have to be playing at the top end of the division. But Bayern and Dortmund are juggernauts of organisations and football clubs. We like to task ourselves with being disruptors to that. We have to try to do things a little bit differently. We have to try to be more involved, more diligent, more intelligent. We've got to have a clear, defined strategy of what we are trying to achieve, and deliver on that. And we are the youngest team in the Bundesliga, and we have the youngest coach.'

Mitchell is one of the most commended figures in football recruitment. At Leipzig, he continued the club's distinct transfer policy and they are growing rapidly. Then, in the summer of 2020, Mitchell left his role as Red Bull International's technical director and joined French side AS Monaco to aid their rebuild. His work at Leipzig and later on for the group hasn't gone unnoticed. He was heavily involved in the building of the squad that had a positive 2019/20 season both domestically in Europe, whilst also keeping an eye on the international side of things. Bragantino moved up a division to the top flight whilst New York are resurgent. Despite being with the Red Bull group for a short time, Mitchell's efforts have been important.

MENSCHENFÄNGER

'MANAGEMENT IS 30 per cent tactics and 70 per cent social competence,' says Julian Nagelsmann. Dubbed as a '*menschenfänger*', a coach with extraordinary human qualities who can inspire players to reach their maximum potential, Nagelsmann's age has always been under the spotlight. It is something he has taken in his stride and he has built a solid relationship with his players wherever he has been. 'Being young can help [as a manager]. You speak the same language as the players. You know Instagram, Facebook. It's a bit easier to have fun if you're nearly the same age. You know what the players laugh about. They need to have that feeling that he is a cool, funny guy. I can make my jokes.'

Tales of his age have always followed him. He broke barriers by becoming the youngest coach in the Bundesliga, then the Champions League, and the way his career is going, more records will tumble. For the German, though, age is just a number. His ability to devise a beautiful game plan on the pitch as well as the natural connection and rapport he develops with his team off the pitch is something encouraged by his own experiences. Modern football is about more than just what happens on the field of play and Nagelsmann, the brightest talent in present-day coaching, has defied his years and excelled in both aspects.

Nagelsmann was another to challenge the status quo. In the modern era, José Mourinho is the biggest example of the fact that top managers don't necessarily have to have been competent players in the past, and the young German has added weight to this relatively unchallenged belief. It wasn't that Nagelsmann didn't try to become a professional footballer, it was bad luck that had a massive role to play in his on-pitch career. Born in Landsberg am Lech, Bavaria, the talented centre-half joined 1860 Munich at the age of 15. Highly regarded at a club that had a reputation for giving youngsters a chance, it was injuries that stole what was expected to be a bright career. A botched knee operation at the age of 20 ended Nagelsmann's dreams of making it professionally, and the ones closest to him could only wonder just how far he could've gone. Soon after, another crushing blow struck a reeling Nagelsmann. His father, Erwin, died after a short battle with illness and so Julian needed to rebuild: first mentally, and then professionally.

There were doubts over whether he wanted to continue in the game, but those were quickly erased. His football journey would continue, albeit with a bit of education in between. Nagelsmann exchanged the pitch for the classroom and the playing route for the academic route. Four semesters at university, initially with a business degree before switching to pursue sports science, put the persistent Nagelsmann in a good position for his return to the game. Then, he also worked on his coaching licence, achieving an A grade. Nagelsmann had all the hallmarks of a great football mind. As a player, he had been highly rated at 1860 Munich. A 6ft 2in centre-half who modelled his style around John Terry, he was a beloved figure in the dressing room for his sense of humour and connection with his team-mates. His human characteristics combined with his rapid ability to learn things and the strong mentality which enabled him to recover from two life-changing tragedies early in his life meant that his return to football was hardly surprising.

Nagelsmann would join Augsburg to work under Thomas Tuchel, who was starting to make a name for himself in the Bundesliga. It was Tuchel who gave Nagelsmann a good recommendation whilst the latter was working on his coaching badges. Working with the club's youth sides and often joining and learning from Tuchel, who was in charge of the senior team, this was a good place to make his break in coaching. Soon, in 2010, Nagelsmann would jump ship, moving to Hoffenheim where he would continue to build experience in the academy. Hoffenheim, at the time, were led by the revolutionary Ralf Rangnick, the man who changed the ideology around the club. He instantly took notice of Nagelsmann, as the Bavarian native steadily progressed from the U-16s to the U-19s championship in 2014. Rangnick joined Red Bull in 2012 and wished to give the academy coach a shot at the first team at Red Bull Salzburg, but a move never materialised.

The U-19 championship enriched Nagelsmann's standing at Hoffenheim, with Bayern Munich keen on bringing him back to Bavaria as part of their academy. Bayern did their best to tempt Nagelsmann, inviting him over to Säbener Straße where chairman Karl-Heinz Rummenigge and sporting director Matthias Sammer showed him around. Pep Guardiola even had a little chat with him, but Nagelsmann could not be lured away.

To protect their brightest prospect, 'Die Kraichgauer' formulated a plan that would see Nagelsmann take charge of the senior team ahead of the 2016/17 season. However, a dreadful campaign before that saw Hoffenheim battling relegation and head coach Huub Stevens decided to leave his role in February 2016, citing heart issues throughout the winter. Nagelsmann got his promotion five months in advance and, to much disbelief, the 28-year-old became the youngest coach in Bundesliga history. Branded as a mere PR stunt by local papers, the effect Nagelsmann had was stunning. When he took over, Hoffenheim were 17th in the league, seven points from safety, and by the end, they managed to stay up, winning seven of their remaining 14 matches and finishing in 15th, a point and a place above the relegation play-off spot.

Over the next three seasons, Nagelsmann would make Hoffenheim one of Germany's most exciting teams. This wasn't a squad that consisted of world beaters, but they had the mentality to get to the very top and, led by a coach who was just as hungry to make a name for himself, they had the right blend. The coach would put to good use his early wisdom about how to drive his players forward and would also use billionaire owner Dietmar Hopp's money to good effect by installing some advanced technology. Hoffenheim used Footbonaut, a square-shaped enclosure where footballs are drilled at players who must control and then pass back through a target area. Additionally, Nagelsmann would request the installation of the unique Videowall at the club's training ground. This is a system of cameras, one behind each goal and two overlooking the central area, controlled by his coaching staff and replayed on to a 6 x 3m screen positioned on the halfway line of their main pitch, giving Nagelsmann the chance to explain situations in training in far more detail.

This technological influence certainly gave Hoffenheim an edge, but Nagelsmann's tactical nous was excellent as well. Picking up points from his mentor Tuchel, the father of modern German pressing, Rangnick, and one of his coaching idols, Pep Guardiola, he was a thorough tactician. With the ability to be flexible, the German mostly worked around a 3-1-4-2 formation, with variations according to the opposition. A key cog in this well-oiled machine was Kevin Vogt, who signed from Köln as a central-midfielder in Nagelsmann's first transfer window. He was converted to the core of the three-man defence, as his supreme ball-playing abilities made him a good connection between defence and midfield. Defined by his coach as the team's quarterback, he was the most crucial element in the backline. The centre-backs were given the freedom to advance into spaces to then work a pass or build up play by breaking through lines.

Hoffenheim's positional play and organisation was also exquisite. The two wing-backs would stretch play as widely as possible and they would be aided by the central-midfielders, who not only occupied the central spaces on the pitch, but also pushed up wide very often. This would enable them to combine with the forwards or supporting wing-backs to create overloads on the opposition in dangerous areas of the pitch. Serge Gnabry, who joined the Sinsheim club on loan for the 2017/18 season, enjoyed working in this system. His shrewd movement and the extra space earned as a result of his team's collective excellence allowed him to weave his magic as his successful loan spell saw him net ten goals in 26 appearances across all competitions and make his way into Germany's senior team.

The 3-1-4-2 and increased work on their pressing patterns allowed the creation of the *'pendeleffekt'*, or the 'pendulum effect', which essentially meant that if Hoffenheim were attacked on one side, the players would move across from the opposite side and build up more resistance in their press, while withdrawing the intensity from the flank they moved away from for stability. Their man-oriented pressing styles would also see the forwards get involved in pressing opposition backlines and try to force as many errors as possible by pushing up to mark opposing centre-halves with a midfielder supporting them. Over the course of his three-and-a-half-year spell at the club, Nagelsmann would develop and work with plenty of efficient and reliable forwards and goalscorers, including Ishak Belfodil, Mark Uth, Andrej Kramarić, Sandro Wagner and Joelinton.

Having joined as part of the laptop trainer revolution that would see coaches, who were as young as players, take charge of squads, Nagelsmann's impact in the Bundesliga, where he provided a different dimension to Guardiola's positioning and ball retention philosophies as well as Rangnick and Tuchel's pressing ideas, made him one of the most acclaimed coaches in Europe. After the miraculous survival in 2016, Hoffenheim continued their strong form from the previous season and, as the team improved, so did the emerging Nagelsmann. His training methods were more refined, team-talks became more succinct, he was attempting newer things, and this only added to his development as a person and as a coach. 'I work like a baker,' he says, 'I mix things, put them in the oven and see if I like what comes out.' From relegation favourites 12 months prior, Hoffenheim finished fourth in 2017, qualifying for the Champions League play-offs.

They wouldn't make the group stages, falling to Jürgen Klopp's Liverpool, but Nagelsmann and Hoffenheim weren't deterred. Despite losing important names like Sebastian Rudy, Niklas Süle and Wagner over the next season, their form would continue. The club would finish in third, continuing a historic run that had been unthinkable not too long before. Losing players was not a problem; the faith Nagelsmann had in his own abilities as well as the improvement of names like Kerem Demirbay and Nico Schulz saw them defy all expectations. At the end of the season, he received a call from Real Madrid's José Ángel Sánchez, who wanted the German to replace the departing Zinedine Zidane, but it was an idea Nagelsmann rejected.

Speaking to *The Independent* about it, he said: 'It's normal if Real Madrid call you, you think about it. I was surprised at first, I weighed it up and I didn't feel comfortable with a decision to go there. I want to improve. If you go to Real Madrid, there's no time to improve as a manager. You don't have a chance to be a better manager, you already have to be the best. I'm not the best now, but I can admit I want to be one of the best in future. If you go to Real Madrid or Barcelona, the fans, the media and the decision-makers don't give you the time to grow into that. They only want to see victories every game, titles, Champions League trophies. If you don't win, you can't say, "But I'm still young, I'm still developing."

It's not that easy in football to plan a career, because it is so unpredictable, but you have to try. The main thing is to make the right steps, not the biggest steps. Madrid is probably one of the highest steps you can take so I thought, "You turn 31, go to Real and where to do you go from there?"'

He would, however, enter an agreement with RB Leipzig that would see him join in the 2019/20 season, meaning he had one more campaign to achieve great things in Sinsheim. This campaign would be the most underwhelming – particularly in the Champions League. Making their debut in the competition proper, Hoffenheim finished bottom of the group, a run that included two defeats to Guardiola's Manchester City. The intensity of Nagelsmann's training sessions was just not suitable for players to do well in two high-quality competitions. Training was of utmost importance and the financial investment in personnel was just not adequate to build a squad capable of handling major tournaments. Much like Rangnick, Nagelsmann desires a certain level of control over how things are done but in his final season at Hoffenheim, it was noticeable that the team was not good enough to compete at their best in the Bundesliga and Champions League. The club finished ninth in the league, but the coach's reputation was still strong – he had a bright future waiting.

Nagelsmann departed with an exceptional record: over the course of 116 Bundesliga matches, Hoffenheim had picked up 191 points, behind Bayern Munich (279) and Borussia Dortmund (228), whilst finishing ahead of traditional giants Schalke, Bayer Leverkusen and Borussia Mönchengladbach. With some of the biggest clubs after his signature, why did Nagelsmann choose RB Leipzig?

Primarily, a move like this was seen as natural progression. Having started at a mid-table club and taken them to the Champions League, it seemed right to move to a club that was a level above, one that was pushing to challenge Bayern Munich for the title but wasn't yet fully established in the upper echelons of German and European football. As Nagelsmann himself put it, a move to Real Madrid or any of Europe's elite would've been skipping a few steps and perhaps even interfering with his own development – that was less likely to happen at Leipzig, especially with the structures they have in place. In the future, there will certainly be chances for him to make a big move.

Secondly, he was joining a club with similar ambitions. Like Rangnick moving from Hoffenheim to Leipzig and getting significant control over operations, Nagelsmann wanted the same to an extent. Prior to his arrival, Leipzig had been performing consistently in ways that would suit his style of management and he was happy with his decision, as he explained in his first press conference: 'I love clubs where a philosophy is set and the coach doesn't have to set the philosophy,' he said with a grin.

At Leipzig's training camp in Seefeld, Austria, the players got an idea of what they were in for after just one session. Nagelsmann, overseeing training from up in the air by standing on a platform lifted by a crane, made it clear he wanted his team's structure to be more coherent and his forwards pushing higher up the pitch. Like at Hoffenheim, he called for intensity, meticulously preparing counter-pressing drills and innovating plans to ready his team in order to do well in three competitions. He saw Leipzig as a step up and he wanted to back that with results on the pitch. Immediately, defender Marcel Halstenberg noted the differences: 'It is very demanding. You also have to think about it calmly when it comes to the game forms [training drills]. I think we haven't even had two identical forms of play.'

Leipzig, who had undergone a restructuring in the summer, not only with the coach but also with new sporting director Markus Krösche, were under pressure early in the season. After heavy defeats to FC Zürich and Aston Villa at home in pre-season as well as an unconvincing cup win over their second-division neighbours VfL Osnabrück, a response was needed. That came in the form of a near-flawless start in the league as they won four of their opening five, drawing against Bayern before defeat to Schalke. The next few weeks were tough, dropping points against Leverkusen, Wolfsburg and Freiburg. In reply, Nagelsmann's team achieved the biggest win in their history, thrashing Mainz 8-0 at home, with Timo Werner bagging a hat-trick of goals and assists.

Goals flowed freely in this team, as they netted 34 times across eight matches (including the Mainz game) between early November and mid-January, winning all but one of the matches in this period, and drawing the other, 3-3 against Borussia Dortmund. Sitting on top of the Bundesliga, both coach and club overcame their Champions League demons by winning a group consisting of Lyon, Benfica and Zenit St Petersburg. Leipzig had never reached this far; Nagelsmann became the youngest coach to ever do so.

A slump in the second half of the season followed and saw Bayern return to the top of the table, but there was one week in February 2020 that showed the best of this Leipzig team. It started with an unsurprising 3-0 home win over Werder Bremen, proceeded to a 1-0 away success over Tottenham in the Champions League – a very flattering scoreline from Tottenham's perspective, relative to Leipzig's impressive performance – and then concluded with a 5-0 away thumping of Schalke, arguably the most dominant display by any team in Europe's top five leagues. The match in Gelsenkirchen came just three days after 'Die Roten Bullen's' trip to London, and Leipzig were untouchable, covering six kilometres more ground than their rivals despite a more demanding schedule. Some three weeks later, they would finish the European job, dispatching Spurs 3-0 with ease and qualifying for the last eight, before the COVID-19 pandemic halted football.

Red Bull Salzburg's early years saw plenty of managers take the reins. Giovanni Trapattoni was one of them.

Starting their football operations in Germany was a milestone for Red Bull. Leipzig started life from the fifth division and got a lot more attention than normally given to a club that low.

Thierry Henry was one of many stars that moved to Major League Soccer with the New York Red Bulls.

No person has been more important to Red Bull's football empire than Ralf Rangnick.

Red Bull's far-reaching scouting network has seen them acquire some of the finest talent from around the world – Sadio Mané is one example.

Jesse Marsch has had a role at three Red Bull clubs – head coach at New York and Salzburg; assistant at Leipzig.

There are several similarities between Julian Nagelsmann and Ralf Rangnick. The young manager's move to Leipzig was a natural progression.

Red Bull Bragantino were saved as a club in 2019 and made it to the top flight of Brazilian football that year.

Sebastian Vettel won the Formula 1 world championship as a Red Bull driver before moving to Ferrari. His legacy is expected to be carried forward by Max Verstappen.

Leipzig's presence in the Bundesliga is not welcomed by many. Borussia Dortmund have been one of the most vocal clubs in that regard.

Ralph Hasenhüttl was seen as the ideal man to take Leipzig forward when they were promoted to the Bundesliga. They finished second in his first season.

Leipzig and Salzburg squared off in a competitive match for the first time in the Europa League in 2018.

Marco Rose and René Marić are an ideal example of the Red Bull model. They were given the senior roles at Red Bull Salzburg having been successful with the youth teams in prior years.

Making the best use of their talents, promoting from within and maintaining efficiency are key philosophies for all Red Bull clubs.

Bradley Wright-Phillips, the New York Red Bulls' greatest forward.

Jürgen Klopp is an admirer of Red Bull's work. He has signed three Red Bull alumni since he joined Liverpool in 2016: Sadio Mané, Naby Keïta and Takumi Minamino.

Leipzig's domestic form after the break was patchy, adding to the problems they faced in the second half of the 2019/20 campaign. Nagelsmann's team ended up finishing third in the Bundesliga behind Bayern Munich and Borussia Dortmund, which was by no means a negative result, but considering they had been in a strong position at the top during the winter, more had been expected from them. Their form after the restart exemplified their slump: four wins, four draws and one loss, very nearly missing out on Champions League football for the 2020/21 campaign.

In Europe, however, they pulled off a shock victory over Diego Simeone's fancied Atlético Madrid, mastering their Spanish opponents for the most part with their energy. They took the lead, conceded an equaliser and didn't back down, as Tyler Adams scored a late winner. 'A gigantic evening that will last in our memories forever,' said a jubilant Halsenberg after the game. As one of the more senior members and one who had been around since they were in the second division, this was a huge moment in his and the team-mates' careers as they celebrated joyously. The next day, they were back at work, as a tougher challenge awaited.

The semi-final set up a tie with someone Nagelsmann knew well – Tuchel's Paris Saint-Germain – as both sides fought it out to make it to the Champions League Final for the very first time.

A match against Tuchel was fitting. Both coaches played as defenders, both had their playing days cut short by injuries, both started coaching in their 20s and both were heavily influenced by Rangnick in their careers. On the pitch, PSG were far too good as an error-ridden Leipzig struggled and lost 3-0 in Lisbon. It was still a fine achievement, first for Nagelsmann, who at 33, became the youngest coach to reach a Champions League Final and, secondly, for the club, who reached this stage with a small history in Continental competition. They were yet to play the likes of Real Madrid, Liverpool and Juventus and yet to visit historic venues like the Camp Nou, Old Trafford or San Siro, and yet, here they were, a win away from Europe's biggest game.

The most exciting player in this team was Werner, their all-time top-scorer. The forward's role drastically changed under Nagelsmann, giving him greater freedom by frequently switching to the wing – normally the left – to earn more space and create goalscoring opportunities either for himself or his team-mates, using his intelligence and pace. His clever movement was also beneficial during Leipzig's blistering counter-attacks, dragging himself away from opposition defenders and finding spaces where he could be most devastating. The improved flexibility and careful decision-making led to his best season. He ended it with a good tally of 32 goals – 11 more than his previous best at the club. A move to Chelsea at the end of the campaign was fully deserved.

Another area of improvement was Leipzig's set-pieces. In the Bundesliga alone, they managed more goals from set-pieces than any other team: 20. That came down to four main reasons:

- Dangerous takers: Christopher Nkunku and Angeliño are dangerous from corners and wide free kicks; Marcel Sabitzer is an excellent long-range striker of the ball;
- Leipzig form clusters in the box during corners and wide free kicks to cause havoc and stand in front of the opponents at the time of delivery;
- The diagonal movements within the box and crossing movements from corners and wide free kicks often distract markers;
- Leipzig's penalty record was superb: they didn't miss one all season.

The season saw plenty of players go from strength to strength. The likes of Halstenberg and Lukas Klostermann improved in the injury-induced absences of Willi Orban and Ibrahima

Konaté; Patrik Schick, Nkunku and Angeliño, unwanted at their previous clubs, became integral parts of this team; Werner, Sabitzer and Dayot Upamecano, players chased by some of Europe's best, performed as though there was no pressure. There may have been no silverware at the end of Nagelsmann's first campaign, but the foundations were certainly laid for future success. No scene will enhance Red Bull's footballing empire more than Leipzig winning the Bundesliga and, under Nagelsmann, they seem best equipped to lift the *Meisterschale* and shock the system in Germany.

Nagelsmann, when asked what he believed beautiful football is: 'Basically offensive football. You shouldn't be too defensive, and you need to try to inspire the spectators. The players should have fun with what they do on the field. A game should be like a concert – it should entertain the people. On top of that should be the success – without that it doesn't work.'

Two clubs at 33 years old and a reputation in gold, Nagelsmann is the future of German coaching. A football coach who skateboards his way to and from work and is currently training for a pilot's licence for small aircraft, rather unsurprisingly doesn't see a long future in the game for himself, with plans to call time by 50 if he is successful, with the aim of living a normal life in the Alps as a mountain guide. For at least the next 17 years, though, Nagelsmann's genius can be cherished. Leipzig had enormous faith in him when they gave him the reins and he has repaid that to an extent; now, it's time for the next step.

For Nagelsmann, football isn't everything – there is more to life than a 70cm air-filled sphere and he wants elements of his life away from the game to resonate amongst his players as well, because the benefits of that can contribute to their primary roles on the pitch. 'No mobile, no WhatsApp, no meetings,' he told the *Daily Mail* about his extreme hobbies, which see him go out to Leipzig's peaks. 'It's a beautiful landscape. I feel free. You can breathe deeply. You feel smaller. These help me avoid bad days. You can't just have football, football, football. If you love other things, it will always be a pleasure to be on the pitch.' When he and his team are on the pitch, however, he will give it his best to be the best.

A PROMISE TO MY FATHER

'I'VE BEEN president for 22 years. It's a big thrill. Any Brazilian club would want this, and we managed to bring it to Bragança. I'm keeping a promise to my father. Before he died, he asked me to not let Bragantino die – and Bragantino with Red Bull eternalise that,' said an emotional Marquinho Chedid, after the renewed Bragantino won promotion to the Brazilian top flight at the tail end of 2019. This was an immense achievement for a club that had been struggling to survive just a year prior to their partnership with the energy drinks giant, and the joy reverberated amongst everyone associated with them.

Bragantino don't have the greatest history, but what little they can stake claim to, is of great value. Formerly known as Clube Atlético Bragantino, who were founded in 1928, they were a modest little club in São Paulo. In 1989, under the management of Vanderlei Luxemburgo, whose CV included a host of local clubs, the Brazilian national team and later Real Madrid, they won the second division before claiming the São Paulo state championship the following year. Funded by Nabi Abi Chedid, the president of the club from 1958 until 1997 and the head of the Brazilian Football Confederation between 1986 and 1989, they were in good hands. Two years after the second-division glory, Bragantino would reach the final of the national championship under the tutelage of Carlos Alberto

Parreira, the future World Cup winner, losing to Telê Santana's São Paulo.

These golden days wouldn't last long. After Chedid Sr departed his role in the late '90s and his son, Marquinho took over, the club endured a rough patch, with financial trouble, dwindling attendances and a stadium which lacked atmosphere. They were preparing for another campaign in Série B in 2019 when a deal was struck with Red Bull that would see them take a different direction for the future.

Red Bull themselves already had a presence in Brazilian football, albeit not a glittering one. In 2007, after successful takeovers and rebrandings in Salzburg and New York, they set their sights on the South American nation with the aim of developing young players whilst getting significant experience in a good environment. Brazil produces a never-ending line of talented footballers and it was only natural that they would tap into that – the famous saying, 'it's easier to sell a crap Brazilian than a brilliant Mexican' shows that the interest in Brazilian footballers has always been there. With that in mind, Red Bull Brasil was born.

However, the complicated Brazilian league system meant that Red Bull Brasil never got out of the São Paulo state leagues – only going as far as the fourth tier, Série D. They also faced major issues in terms of fan interest; they had the structure and resources, but failed to fill up their stadium. A large reason for this was that they were based in a region with two historic Brazilian clubs, Ponte Preta and Guarani, who attracted the majority share of the fans. In a city so divided between two traditional clubs, when the third came, few people paid attention. The average attendances for Red Bull Brasil games were strikingly low, despite it being a hopeful project. With the ambition to continue their work in the country and the institutional changes at Red Bull International Soccer (which would see Ralf Rangnick and Paul Mitchell's responsibilities change), the company identified Bragantino.

With Red Bull's investment in Bragantino, there was a lot of curiosity over how the club would be managed. Football clubs in Brazil are usually in financial difficulties, with players often being paid their salaries months behind schedule – even by those clubs at the top of the footballing pyramid. Knowing Red Bull's cohesive investments in Europe and the United States of America, there was excitement that Bragantino, after years of struggle, would receive long-term and well-planned funding and, from a neutral's perspective, there was hope that more local clubs would follow. Despite some criticism, including a few publications in the country labelling the club as a 'businessman's team', they were regarded as a breath of fresh air.

Red Bull first contacted Bragantino in late December 2018 and by the following March a deal was completed. There were a few compromises made in talks between the two parties. Unlike the two European sides and the Red Bulls in MLS, there was no changing of history: Bragantino kept their white home and black away strips, although they would have two bulls adorning the midriff. There was also an agreement that, unlike Markranstädt's transition to RB Leipzig and the MetroStars' conversion to the New York Red Bulls, the name Bragantino would be kept in some respect. Red Bull then laid out a plan that would see the crest and name remain the same for the 2019 season, before changing to a different logo – one like the other clubs in the umbrella – and the name going from Clube Atlético Bragantino to Red Bull Bragantino. These changes were widely accepted by the fans, who now had revitalised belief in seeing their team do well and achieving things on the pitch.

The company's objective in Brazil was to fast-track their way through to the top flight and give their players a more competitive experience – something they had failed to do with Red Bull Brasil, who would play in the Campeonato Paulista Série A2, the second level of the São Paulo state championship, where they would act as the developmental team for Bragantino.

To help them make their way to the first division as quickly as possible, Red Bull Brasil gave Bragantino their best players ahead of the season and the club now had a boost in quality which showed in their results. The core of the team were players who had had impressive careers.

Guarding the goal was the skilled Júlio César, who previously played over 130 times for Corinthians and was a part of the team that won the Copa Libertadores and FIFA Club World Cup in 2012. He represented Red Bull Brasil in 2018 and 2019, before moving to Bragantino. In front of him stood Léo Ortiz, formerly of Internacional, and Ligger, who represented Fortaleza. The two would form a stern pairing at the back. Leading the attack were Claudinho, a tricky winger and arguably the most entertaining player in the team, and forward Ytalo, who had had opportunities in Europe, even scoring a Europa League goal for Macedonian club FK Vardar. Together, this team would blow away the competition in the second tier.

Seven matches into the season, Bragantino, coached by Antônio Carlos Zago, whose CV included spells at AS Roma and Shakhtar Donetsk as an assistant, were sitting on top of the league and they went all the way from there. After a comfortable 3-0 win over Atlético Goianiense in the third week of the season, interest in the team rose as more fans took notice of the good football being played. More positive results followed as the team marched towards promotion. Claudinho was widely regarded as the best player in the division, with his desire and ability to dazzle making him a favourite of the crowd.

One criticism of Bragantino in a near-perfect season would be of their failure to beat teams close to them. When squaring off against the three teams promoted with them, Sport, Coritiba and Atlético Goianiense, they only picked up six out of a possible 18 points – half of which came from the win against Goianiense. However, Bragantino would take pride from the fact that they were comfortable in most other games. The team enjoyed a come-from-behind 2 1 success over Ponte Preta in July and then later in November against Guarani by three goals to one, after which they were confirmed as being promoted. By the end, Bragantino won the league by scoring the most goals in the division, conceding the fewest and enjoying a seven-point gap over Sport. This was a season that showed the players' strengths and Red Bull's ambition to right the wrongs of their previous interests in Brazil.

Reaching Série A was the first step, but Bragantino and Red Bull had a series of long-term goals that not only envisaged them dominating Brazilian football but making an impact across South America as well. Speaking to *Globo Esporte* after winning promotion, the club's executive director Thiago Scuro laid out their vision for the future: 'I have no doubt that in three years Bragantino will be competing at the top of the table. Before those three years comes 2020. In 2020, the challenge is huge because we're moving up from Série B to Série A, and for any team that goes up, the first goal is to stay. That's the main goal of the season, that's the reality. At the same time, we're investing in players who tend to be better every season, in a team that tends to perform collectively better every year. Investment in infrastructure, in new professionals, in technology: it's a challenging process, especially because of the rapid growth of the club.'

Ahead of the 2020 season in the top flight, Bragantino made some huge investments to bolster their playing squad. In the transfer window, they spent R$125m (approximately €19.35m), the third-most behind the Brazilian and South American champions Flamengo and Palmeiras, who spent €47m and €21m respectively. It was in this window that Red Bull established their blueprint of bringing in gifted youngsters to develop. The club's most expensive signing was 21-year-old forward Arthur, who joined for R$25m from Palmeiras. He was joined by two Atlético Mineiro players: goalkeeper Cleiton (22 years old, R$23m) and forward Alerrandro (20, R$14m).

Bragantino also signed two names from one of Brazil's biggest clubs, Grêmio, with defender Thonny Anderson (22, R$13m) and Weverton, a creative midfielder (20 R$5m) joining.

The average age of all of Bragantino's signings was just 23.5 years old and they were all brought in from clubs that had a huge reputation in developing Brazilian stars. Red Bull also used their internal connections to good effect. RB Leipzig signed left-back Luan Cândido in the summer of 2019, before he even debuted for Palmeiras. They gave him the chance to get accustomed to European football and lifestyle, before being loaned out to Bragantino in the winter, just ahead of the start of the Brazilian season. With Red Bull now paying more attention to the international set-ups in New York and Brazil, there is no doubt that more names will be crossing borders in the future.

The investment wasn't just restricted to the players. Bragantino laid out plans for modernising their stadium, converting it to a 20,000-seater arena by 2021. Their current venue, Estádio Nabi Abi Chedid, also known as Nabizão, is old and unsafe with fans sitting on rodeo bleachers and the stadium having a dull and tired look. Over the course of Red Bull's first season of involvement with Bragantino, match attendances had significantly increased, going from a few hundred to several thousand, and to accommodate that interest, a modern stadium, complete with necessary services for fans, such as better concession offerings and accessible parking spaces, was essential. Bragantino had the fourth-highest average attendance figures (6,207 fans per game) in Série B – big ambitions needed the infrastructure to match.

In addition to that, there are also plans for a new training facility closer to the city. Bragantino currently train at a centre about 50km away, but the new venue, complete with eight full-sized pitches and state-of-the-art equipment, is set to raise the club's standing. This was just what fans had expected when the news of Red Bull's takeover was made public. Short-term betterment doesn't do the club any good – making long-term changes that aren't restricted solely to on-pitch investment can change the feel of the club, get players more interested in joining and create more engagement with fans and the local community. They've also given greater attention towards their women's team, appointing Camilla Orlando, a renowned coach at youth level, as the woman to lead the new first team.

The increased investment in facilities was also something backed by the local authorities. The deputy mayor of Bragança Paulista (the municipality where Bragantino are based), Amauri Sodré, has spoken of his pleasure in seeing a rise in hotel bookings, visits to restaurants, bars and petrol stations and has declared he will continue to back Bragantino and Red Bull's projects as much as possible.

Scuro is also delighted with the impact the club has had amongst fans in the city: 'The enthusiasm of the fans is outstanding. It's nice to see the anxiety, the expectation. But it's important to remember that our biggest crowd [attending a match] was in the first round, when we had zero points. That shows how important the city and the fans were and that they wanted to be part of this project.' The fan support was evident at the club's promotion celebrations as well, with hundreds queuing up to buy a special-edition commemorative Red Bull shirt with no qualms.

Another huge positive going for Red Bull's operations in Brazil is the presence of Red Bull Brasil as the feeder club and their good run of results. They did well in the U-20 cup in 2019 and provide a good learning ground for players to adapt to the Red Bull model. In addition to a U-23 team playing in the São Paulo state championship, they actively take part in various cup competitions, giving younger players a chance to find their way to the Brazilian top flight with Bragantino.

There was one issue for Bragantino ahead of the 2020 campaign as coach Zago left for Japan's Kashima Antlers. He was replaced by Felipe Conceição, the 41-year-old former forward who previously led Botafogo and América Mineiro.

Despite the change, Bragantino are optimistic about the future. The convoluted Brazilian league system often sees players depart at early ages, coaches constantly sacked and replaced and clubs suffering from dire financial conditions. There is also the fact that the league calendar isn't aligned with the European football calendar, whose summer transfer window clashes with the midway point of Brazil's season, meaning many players jump ship then, making the management and long-term planning for clubs in the country even more difficult. However, Bragantino wish to be an exception to that. There is belief that the club could become a model for others to follow and if they are successful, they can change the outlook towards Brazilian domestic football and how it operates.

Scuro: 'Red Bull have very big performance expectations. The goal of the Formula 1 team is to win races. The goal of the football clubs is to win championships. We're very encouraged to do that and that's it. All this contributes to the growth of the brand, so that people have a healthier relationship with the brand, everyone likes to win and to feel the pleasure [of winning]. The more we win, the more people will join the brand. It is a natural process of linking the club with the product [the beverage]. We don't have any kind of goal or link to the product and how it performs in the market – that's another management, another area. Our goal is to build a strong, victorious Bragantino so that it can provide emotions for people. This is the great difference between Red Bull's investment in sports [and other ventures by the company]. It works to win in whatever it does.' As Scuro puts it, Red Bull are here to stay, and Bragantino will fly their flag in Brazil. Good days are not far away for this ambitious club.

Reference:
Law, J. *Rag to a bull*, When Saturday Comes, Issue 395, February 2020

Transfer data correct as of August 2020

A SPORTING DYNASTY

VERY FEW can match the ambition of Red Bull's goals in sport – it is perhaps something that has never been seen before. The energy drink company, inspired by their eccentric owner Dietrich Mateschitz, have been revolutionary when it comes to sport, and their constant search for thrill, adrenaline and excitement has reaped vast rewards, not only for themselves, but also for all the teams and athletes associated with them. Whilst their football investments garner the most attention, Red Bull's operations across a variety of sports display the scale of their resolve – this company knows no boundaries.

In the early days of their distinct guerrilla marketing strategies, Red Bull advertising hoardings were visible at extreme sports events, ranging from skiing to flying to skateboarding. Nigel Mansell, the former Formula 1 champion, was the first sponsored athlete but it wasn't until the 1996 Summer Olympics in Atlanta that they started to gain more attention for their sporting ventures. Xeno Müller, Switzerland's single scull gold medallist, was a Red Bull athlete too. Soon, the company would start to become a more mainstream name in the sporting world and would go beyond just sponsorship deals. Towards the end of the '90s and the turn of the century, they would organise their own high-energy, creative events such as the Red Bull SoapBox Race and the Red Bull Air Race, as they became a well-known entity in extreme sports.

As the decade progressed, their involvement rose and their affinity towards extreme increased. The main reasons for the company's adventurous modus operandi were down to their origins. Firstly, being from Austria where sports like these have an immense standing, it's only natural that they followed suit. Some of the great Austrian sportspeople in history include alpine skiers like Hermann Maier and Annemarie Moser-Pröll whilst others such as Armin Kogler (ski jumping) and Anne Gasser (snowboarding) have taken advantage of the country's natural offerings. To add to that, Red Bull's own target demographic, as explained earlier, are 18 to 34-year-old daredevils who need something they can resonate with. Red Bull events heavily feature company marketing, and as their popularity grew, their promotion grew, with banners and trucks displaying the famous two bulls all over the place.

Most of this might be disregarded as mere marketing ploys, but Red Bull's commitment to continuously improve and keep pushing their bold instincts has worked a treat. They create credibility through their catchy yet emotionally appealing styles, stimulating people's desire for adventure and athletes' inner drive. Combine that with their image, their impulse to promote what they do through their use of media and their will to always be out there, and that explains exactly why they are so successful. Over the years they have backed excellent athletes who have won Olympic medals, world championships and adulation from the world over.

Recent times have seen them work closely with some of the biggest names in outdoor sports such as skiing legend Lindsey Vonn, slopestyle icon Mark McMorris and a number of athletes who have participated at both the summer and winter Olympics. There have been plenty of Red Bull athletes in each of the last three Winter Olympic Games, with 16 winning medals in 2010 in Vancouver. If Red Bull were a nation, their tally that year would've seen them finish fifth in the overall medals table. 'We don't focus on the Olympics per se,' says Andy Walshe, Red

Bull's director of high performance to *Men's Journal*. 'A lot of our sports have just been absorbed into the Olympic portfolio.'

Walshe's role in the Red Bull sporting machine is of paramount importance. The Australian joined in 2007 after nearly a decade with the US ski team during its most successful years and he revolutionised the Red Bull way, shifting towards more sport and less marketing.

No event highlights their strategies better than Felix Baumgartner's record-breaking space jump. On the morning of 14 October 2012, the 43-year-old Austrian made history by diving from nearly 128,000 feet up in the air, breaking the record for a human free-fall and, in the process, the speed of sound.

Red Bull Stratos, as it was known, was a leap that was five years in the making. Baumgartner had priors in jumping, including from the Petronas Towers in Kuala Lumpur and the lowest BASE jump in history at the time, from the hand of the Christ the Redeemer statue in Rio de Janeiro. He went through vigorous training in preparation for his Stratos jump. His two test jumps – conducted from 71,581 feet and 97,145 feet – were crucial rehearsals for what was ahead. The final take, a mighty leap through thin air, was to be historic.

Aided by Joseph Kittenger, a former free-fall record holder from 1960 and officer in the United States Air Force, this feat involved intense planning. On his way up, Baumgartner had to go through a 43-step checklist in order to ensure the jump was as safe as it could be, which included points about his pressure suit, oxygen, air pressure and more. One misstep would've had grave consequences. Months prior to the historic event, Baumgartner had started developing a phobia of the pressure suit which was so severe that he nearly gave up on the project. However, after taking help from psychologist Mike Gervais, he pushed on.

From 127,852 feet, Baumgartner took the leap, reaching a top speed of 844mph. This was the Austrian's crowning moment. Born in Salzburg and having started his jumping career in 1986 at the age of 16, this was what he had been waiting for. All the cliffs, towers and monuments led to this moment in space, with him and him alone enjoying a date with history. Speaking to *Forbes*, he said: 'It was beautiful – I could see the curve of the earth below me, and above, the sky was just black. I'd never seen black sky before. I did try to breathe in that special moment, but at the same time, I was all business. I knew there was only about ten minutes of oxygen on my back, and I couldn't allow myself to become distracted. I had to jump.'

Red Bull took an interest in Baumgartner in 1997, but after his jump from Taiwan's Taipei 101 in 2007, his act began to become stale – how many more towers could he jump from before people stopped paying attention? At that point, instead of retiring, which was a serious option, he had a dream which the company supported. In December 2007, Red Bull agreed to take Baumgartner out of the world for a leap, and then reportedly spent $28m doing so.

The overall cost included engineering, marketing, research and hiring, and for the jump itself, Red Bull made it certain the world knew they were involved by installing nine high-definition cameras, three 4K cameras and three DSLRs, while Baumgartner himself had five GoPro cameras embedded into his pressure suit. The two-and-a-half-hour ascent and 11-minute descent was watched simultaneously by eight million people on YouTube, a record, whilst 80 TV stations in 50 countries broadcasted the event. It was a massive success. Buzz Aldrin, the second man on the moon, joked about the accomplishment: 'One small step for Felix, one giant leap for Red Bull,' he said.

Red Bull Stratos gave the company an idea of expanding their wings even further, to find how far athletes could be pushed in a tough yet rewarding environment. With that in mind, Project Acheron was created, amongst a series of other plans with similar outlooks. Acheron took athletes, led by former US Navy SEALs, on a tour across Patagonia, a region at the southern end of South America, shared by Chile and Argentina. This area mostly comprises the southern section of the Andes mountains along with lakes, fjords and deserts. Several editions have followed with a view to testing athletes' mentality and strength. 'It's not about breaking them,' Walshe said about Acheron to *Wired*. 'That's easy. It was about crafting a learning experience that allowed them into an unknown environment they had to adapt to. We built in elements of military training, doubled down on the science and tried to build a once-in-a-lifetime experience.'

That was followed by the Breath-Hold Camp, designed to teach surfers how to hold their breath for an average of four minutes. As Red Bull identified the success of this, they began to include more extreme sports athletes, ranging from skiers to snowboarders, as they recognised the psychological improvement it brought along. The Breath-Hold Camp inspired the Performing Under Pressure camp, which aimed to push the limits of athletes in order to deal with high-pressure situations through a series of activities such as mindfulness and speed racing.

Away from individual acts of bravery, Red Bull, just like in football, have been changing clubs in ice hockey. They currently have two European ice hockey clubs under their umbrella: EC Red Bull Salzburg and EHC Red Bull München. The team in Salzburg share their facilities with the football side, but their history isn't the most pleasant. Born in 1977 as HC Salzburg, Red Bull got involved in 2000 after several years of inconsistency, name changes and failures. In the 1980s and '90s, they were blessed with some of the greats such as Viktor Schalimov, Greg Holst and Peter Zenahlik, but struggled to make much of an impact. It wasn't until the takeover in the new millennium and the implementation of a modern, attacking style of play that they started progressing, earning promotion to the first division in 2004, winning the title in 2007 and adding seven more domestic and two European honours after that.

Their sister club in Germany were founded in 1998 as HC München 98, quickly going through the ranks in Germany's ice hockey ladder, finding themselves in the Bundesliga, the top flight, by 2010. After a positive start, the club entered deep financial trouble and in 2013, Red Bull would become the sole owner, changing their name and giving the club a new identity. From there onwards, Munich would win three league titles in a row between 2016 and 2018 and even faced Salzburg in Continental competition, winning a two-legged affair in the Champions Hockey League semi-final 3-1 on aggregate. There's a common trend developing, that whatever Red Bull get involved with turns to gold, and that is signified best by their interests in Formula 1 and motorsport, where their influence has been comprehensive.

Red Bull's alliance with F1 teams began in 1995 with a sponsorship deal with Sauber Motorsport, but they took it up a notch nine years later, when they purchased Jaguar Racing from the Ford Motor Company, in the process naming Christian Horner as the team principal. At 31, Horner was the youngest to hold such a role. In 2005, they added to their network by purchasing Minardi and changing their name to Toro Rosso (which became AlphaTauri from the 2020 season onwards), who would act as the feeder squad for younger drivers to work their way up over a period of time. In having two teams and four cars, Red Bull takes up 20 per cent of the grid. They initially brought a fun, relaxed image to F1, keeping in line with their brand and also working closely with young drivers.

Soon, thanks to the money and resources available to them, they were able to attract some of the best talent in engineering and design, such as Adrian Newey, who had previously worked with Williams and McLaren and was often considered as the finest designer in F1. His signing in 2006 was a serious statement of intent and, in 2007, his first car – the RB3 – was revealed. That immediately moved the senior team to the front of the grid, where its presence was important as it proved that one need not be a mighty car manufacturer to be successful. In 2009, Red Bull finished as runners-up in the championship, before going on to win the title for four years in succession after that, with Sebastian Vettel leading the charge. When he claimed his first championship, Vettel was the youngest ever to do so, and since that feat, Red Bull have formed the 'big three' in modern racing along with historical giants Mercedes and Ferrari.

Horner told *Director* in 2018: 'It's all about the environment you create. If you were to compare us with Mercedes or McLaren, for example, there's far less of a corporate environment here. You'll see that 90 per cent of our designers are in jeans and T-shirts. We don't have strict working hours – it's whatever is needed to get the job done ... Allowing innovative people to express their creativity is so important in what we do. We're not a numbers-driven business.'

In a later interview, he spoke about the mentality of continued success, to *Business Insider*: 'When you're on top, if you win a race, you enjoy it for the evening, but by the time you're back in the office on Monday morning, it's about the next event and wanting to build on that performance. It's so fast-moving, this sport, that you're always focused on the next target, you never get the chance to look backwards. There almost becomes a fear of losing, and there becomes an atmosphere of expectancy going into a race.'

Red Bull's F1 philosophy is very much a homegrown one and that is exemplified by Vettel's rise. The German started off at Toro Rosso and won his first race with the team in 2008 at the Italian Grand Prix before moving to Red Bull. All of the Red Bull Racing drivers since 2014 have been youngsters who were supported right through the lower ranks, with the exception of Max Verstappen, who was signed to Toro Rosso in 2015 having not been associated with Red Bull previously. He became the youngest driver to start a Grand Prix at the age of 17 during the 2015 season. They are ruthless about swapping drivers from

Red Bull to Toro Rosso and vice versa – Verstappen made his debut in that fashion, joining the senior team five races into the 2016 season at Daniil Kvyat's expense and famously winning the Spanish Grand Prix on his debut. More recently, Pierre Gasly was dropped in favour of Alex Albon midway through the 2019 season after the former's underwhelming start to the campaign.

On top of that, Red Bull has invested in the sport in other ways. They helped the Austrian Grand Prix return to the F1 calendar after a ten-year absence in 2014. A decade prior, they had purchased the circuit, the A1 Ring, and renamed it as the Red Bull Ring, thus it became their 'home' race. In 2018, Verstappen became the first Red Bull driver to win there before following it up with the same result a year later. The company's philosophy also includes the continuation in promoting the sport as well as their brand worldwide, by running regular car demonstrations using either race drivers or other Red Bull ambassadors. This has led to stunts such as driving an F1 car on the helipad of the Burj Al Arab in Dubai, going through the Rocky Mountains in Colorado and dashing down the snowy slopes of the Kitzbühel in Austria. There is no end to Red Bull's hunt for extreme.

Mateschitz himself has a very hands-off approach when it comes to the F1 team, as long as it follows the philosophy of the brand. He has put people in place that he trusts and, whilst Horner is the team principal who handles the day-to-day running of the team, the owner has a key advisor in the form of fellow Austrian Dr Helmut Marko, who makes the big decisions. It is Marko who runs the driver programme and decides who is driving for which team – he is the person that has the final say on changes. Having someone who makes the hard decisions leaves Horner dealing with the details of managing the team whilst also informing Mateschitz. Horner makes sure Mateschitz feels he is getting value out of the project.

The company's connection to motorsport isn't solely stuck with F1. They have a young driver academy which funds up-

and-coming talents through the ranks, in turn bringing in sponsorship to the junior teams they are racing for. They are also heavily involved in the Australian Supercars Championship, World Rally Championship and MotoGP, where they sponsor racers like Marc Márquez, the Spanish six-time world champion and one of the all-time best. The Red Bull Ring has also hosted MotoGP races. Across the Atlantic, the company attempted to sponsor NASCAR drivers, but withdrew from US motorsport in 2011 before moving on to the Global Rallycross Championship until that folded in 2019.

Staying with sponsorships, the company works extensively to build and maintain ties with elite athletes around the world in a variety of sports. In cricket, they have worked closely with India's KL Rahul and England's 2019 World Cup hero Ben Stokes; in golf, Red Bull are tied with Lexi Thompson, one of the best on the LPGA Tour; local tennis hero Dominic Thiem has been sponsored by Red Bull since 2018, while over in rugby, Jack Nowell joins the list. These are just a few of over 1,500 talents from several disciplines of sport (and e-sports) that are in partnership with the energy drink giant. All of them (and others upon request) have access to the Athlete Performance Centre on the outskirts of Salzburg, where coaches and experts, with the aid of modern technology, offer advice on physiotherapy, nutrition, conditioning and more, whilst also giving them a place to train.

There is also the Red Bull High Performance Centre inside the company's North American Headquarters in Santa Monica, California. This is a 270m² building with the finest equipment for elite training along with a cinema, gaming room and recording studio. Similar to the centre in Salzburg, this venue also has the latest advances in medical and nutritional apparatus, such as a neurological training system, a sensory-performance station and a therapeutic chamber in which the body is subjected to extremely cold temperatures, amongst others.

It is here that many Olympians come to fine-tune their skills, using data, tests and a host of other tools to explore their talent and help them reach the next level. Speaking to *Wired* about his 'hacking talent' ideology, which sees Red Bull explore how far they can possibly test professional athletes, Walshe says: 'We learned that the principles we use for an athlete are applicable if you're an entrepreneur, a parent or a scientist. That's what's behind the idea of hacking talent. I would like to get to a point where we apply the same amount of energy and resources [as] we apply, say, to the world's top football team, to the individuals tackling social problems or scientists trying to cure cancer. That's what drives us.'

Whether it's on a racing track, the hills of the Alps or up in space, Red Bull's efforts in sport are beyond just marketing acts – they are keen on pushing the boundaries of elite sport. Altering history aside, just like in football, they have given teams and individuals an edge, not only improving their own brand, but also building trustworthy relationships with professionals that have played a part in their success. Red Bull's commitment is unlike any other.

BEYOND BORDERS

HAVING TAKEN their football operations to Austria, the United States of America, Brazil and Germany, rumours are always rife about where Red Bull are going to take their resources next. As seen, the Red Bull approach is simple: take over clubs with a relatively low standing and work with them with adequate investment and an eye on the future. Since Salzburg and Leipzig's success over the last decade, plenty of names have been linked to the Austrian company's umbrella, but most fans are resistant, valuing history over change and the potential altering of their club's identity.

Brøndby, the ten-time Danish champions, were reportedly of interest to Red Bull at the start of 2020. The club haven't been Danish league champions since 2005, having fallen behind the likes of København and Midtjylland and fans were happy with keeping it that way if it meant their 55-year history wasn't sold out. Immediately after the rumours were out, the fans voiced their concerns, telling the *Copenhagen Post*: 'Red Bull stands for everything we despise and all we have fought to not become.

'If Red Bull gets involved with Brondby IF, we will not be able to identify with the club as active fans any longer. In Salzburg and Leipzig, we can see how the Austrian money-men have transformed real football clubs into pure business. They have changed logos, colours, stadium names … everything! We will never let that happen to our club.'

They were even willing to take matters into their own hands, buying 135 tickets at a total cost of €3,000 for the 425 million krone (€56m) EuroJackpot. With their potential winnings, the fans wished to buy the club and manage it themselves, rather than see it go to Red Bull. Ambitious, but nothing like that worked out – not the club changing ownership, nor the fans winning the lottery.

Similarly, there was also talk of Red Bull's interest in Portuguese club CD Aves, who have been battling it out in the bottom half of the league table and won their first major trophy, the Taça de Portugal, in 2018, beating Sporting CP in the final. Given Portugal's recent upturn in talent production, which has seen the country's big three, Benfica, Porto and Sporting, gift the rest of Europe some wonderful young footballers such as Bernardo Silva, Bruno Fernandes and João Félix and more, it seemed likely that Red Bull would target the Iberian nation at some point. Coincidentally, *aves* translates to birds, which would fit in perfectly with the company's marketing strategy.

England is another nation brimming with talent and, looking at the market and popularity of its leagues, expanding operations with a view to proceeding to the Premier League would be smart. Dietrich Mateschitz, however, has been reluctant to make the move. In the past, clubs like West Ham United and Nottingham Forest have been brought up as complicated and controversial potential options, but the Red Bull supremo has been cautious, citing UEFA's Financial Fair Play and conflict of interest regulations as potential obstacles.

Ralf Rangnick has been flirting with the idea as well, stating that clubs lower down in the English league system would be more suited: 'If we wanted to expand, only one club in England would make sense. A third-tier league team like maybe Sunderland or Milton Keynes [Dons]. But problems would arise if the club pushed into international business. Then we would have the same situation as with Leipzig and Salzburg, that would not be done because of the UEFA regulations.'

Red Bull previously expanded to Africa when they went to Sogakope and formed Red Bull Ghana in 2008, with the aim of creating a direct pathway to their European sides. Ghana, who have a rich history when it comes to young talent, seemed like the ideal location at the time in a continent that was brimming with talent. Their steady progress on the international and continental stage resulted in the major success of qualification for their first World Cup in 2006, where they made the second round, falling to defending champions Brazil. Additionally, in the African Cup of Nations, they finished third and runners-up in 2008 and 2010 respectively. Growth was there to see and combining that rise in interest with Red Bull's resources was a shrewd move.

The local fans were largely welcoming of Red Bull's involvement. Having seen Hearts of Oak, the club from the capital of Accra, and Asante Kotoko from Kumasi, dominate the league since the 1990s, the chance to witness a change in power and the rise of a potential new champion was an exciting prospect. On the continental stage, Ghana's last success had come in 2000 when Hearts of Oak beat Tunisia's Espérance in the CAF Champions League Final. A tournament mostly dominated by north African clubs, Red Bull's plans of bringing together, developing and succeeding with the finest west African talent were appealing. However, whilst Red Bull were succeeding with their ventures in Salzburg, New York and Leipzig, the project in Sogakope did not go as they had hoped.

A fair amount of mismanagement led to Red Bull Ghana ceasing to exist in 2014, just six years after their foundation. It failed to generate ideal results, first, from a monetary perspective and, secondly, in their objectives of getting more players to Europe. There was belief that the lack of clarity in their vision led to the club's downfall. Players could get an opportunity to play and grow, but, just like any other club in

Ghana, the chance to further their careers by moving abroad was minimal, which frustrated many. Factor in that most of their staff – whether they were coaches or working behind the scenes – were expatriates, and there seemed to have been little understanding of the local surroundings, and that proved to be a major obstacle.

There were some positives to take from it, such as the construction of a small stadium and the improvement in infrastructure. Furthermore, the club's four coaches – Daniel Hiedemann, Henrik Pedersen, Eelco Schattorie, Sipke Hulsoff – who had previous experiences coaching various European outfits, did contribute to some improvement, despite the barriers. Following the club's dissolution, Red Bull didn't entirely end their operations in Ghana. Their Sogakope site, which included two-and-a-half artificial turf fields, one grass field and an education centre, and cost around €5.5m, was taken over by the West African Football Academy Sporting Club (WAFA SC). Formerly known as Fetteh Feyenoord, in cooperation with the Dutch giants from Rotterdam, WAFA SC, with their knowledge of local environment, have done a much better job and have a hand in contributing to the Red Bull empire in Europe. Several WAFA alumni have made their way through the academy and found their place in Europe, some ending up at Red Bull Salzburg or their farm team, FC Liefering. Examples of this are Gideon Mensah, who joined Salzburg from WAFA in 2016 and has been finding his feet in his new environment whilst out on loan at Sturm Graz and Belgian side Zulte Waregem. Still young, the full-back is looking at a good future. There is also Samuel Tetteh, the 24-year-old forward who also moved to Salzburg in 2015 and has done well for himself whilst out on loan at LASK – a club threatening his parent club's domination in the Bundesliga.

Midfielder Majeed Ashimeru is another WAFA alumni and he got opportunities with the Salzburg first team under

Jesse Marsch in the 2019/20 season, contributing to their title-winning team.

Even though things didn't work according to plan, Red Bull managed to get some value out of their investments in Ghana. Their international network, with a youth-centred approach that involves detailed scouting and establishing worldwide connections, is extraordinary. Just like them, there is another who has taken advantage of their resources and wealth and made investments in football on a grander, further-reaching scale: City Football Group (CFG).

Backed by the billions of the Sheikhs of Abu Dhabi, CFG started off with the purchase of Manchester City in 2008, making them one of the best teams in England and playing a part in breaking the traditional top four of rivals Manchester United, Liverpool, Arsenal and Chelsea. Since then, they have added a host of teams from around the world to their network, including Melbourne City FC (Australia), Yokohama F. Marinos (Japan), Montevideo City Torque (Uruguay), Girona (Spain), Sichuan Jiuniu (China), Mumbai City FC (India) and Lommel SK (Belgium), thus, going across continents and opening pathways.

It is in MLS where Red Bull and CFG, two of modern football's biggest antagonists, meet. New York City FC, the MLS arm of CFG, square off against the New York Red Bulls in the budding Hudson River derby. Just like CFG's marquee club, Manchester City, New York City FC followed the same principles early on: a sky-blue shirt, lots of money, big-name signings, plenty of media hype and a slow start to life despite high expectations.

They became the 20th club in MLS in 2015 and immediately moved for three world-renowned names: David Villa, Frank Lampard and Andrea Pirlo, legends in Spain, England and Italy, who took the leap across the ocean as they approached the end of their careers. Now, New York City FC were the talk of the town.

The rivalry between the two franchises stems primarily out of their location. The Red Bulls' stadium in Harrison, New Jersey means that New York City FC are technically the only MLS team based in New York and reminding their rivals of that is a common trend when the two face off. However, New York City FC's base has proven to be problematic in its own way. They still don't play in a soccer-specific stadium, instead, playing at the home of the New York Yankees, the Yankee Stadium, a baseball venue. When that isn't available, the alternative is Citi Field, home of the New York Mets, also a baseball venue. The awkwardness of a soccer pitch being squeezed into a baseball stadium has resulted in opposition coaches and players complaining about the field's dimensions: the club just meet the requirements on their 70 x 110-yard home – the bare minimum required by FIFA.

The Blues have looked at other venues, but due to high land prices and, primarily, a lack of space in New York's five boroughs – Brooklyn, Manhattan, Queens, Staten Island and the Bronx, where the Yankee Stadium is located – this has proven to be a challenging task. They have settled on a location in the Bronx for a new soccer-only stadium, but the foreseeable future will see New York City FC continue in their adopted home. A CONCACAF Champions League game in February 2020 against Costa Rica's San Carlos saw them use the Red Bull Arena due to the unavailability of both baseball venues, much to the annoyance of their fans and the ridicule of their rivals.

This has been just one pillar of a young rivalry. The newer fans, who started supporting the Red Bulls only after the takeover by the Austrian company, have accepted New York City FC as their main rivals over DC United – who were the enemy for the older supporters. On the pitch, the quality has been there and matches between the two are mostly engrossing, improving the status and reputation of MLS.

The first meeting between the two in May 2015 exemplified the passion the fans had. At the Red Bull Arena, a Bradley

Wright-Phillips double secured a 2-1 win as the supporters from both ends brought out the songs, flags and banners to create an intense, passionate atmosphere. The Red Bulls would continue their domination in the duel, winning the next three clashes – the last of which was the most significant match of this story. At the Yankee Stadium in May 2016, the Red Bulls ran riot as doubles from Wright-Phillips and Dax McCarthy, along with goals from Alex Muyl, Gonzalo Verón and Gideon Baah, secured a 7-0 win over the Patrick Vieira-coached outfit. It would take a little over a month for New York City FC to get over that humiliation and achieve their first derby win: one each from Jack Harrison and David Villa secured the bragging rights in town for the first time.

However, joys like that have been short-lived. The Red Bulls have been the dominant side in this emerging rivalry, twice winning 4-0 and once 4-1 since the thumping at the Yankee Stadium, whilst holding a better overall head-to-head record. New York City FC's recent improvements as well as the inconsistencies of the Red Bulls in the transfer market have seen this become a tense scenario in New York's soccer scene, as both teams vie to win their first MLS Cup. Nevertheless, the Red Bulls will feel they have the edge, given their recent Supporters' Shield victories and fresh memories of resounding wins over their local rivals.

Red Bull and CFG have followed similar philosophies in their football ideology, player and coach sharing, transfers and more. Although the Abu Dhabi-funded group have a greater international portfolio of clubs, Red Bull have been meticulous wherever they have been and almost everything they touch turns to gold. These two groups may be the model and inspiration for more private- or state-funded groups in the future, as football's radical commercialisation continues to increase.

Claudio Reyna, who has represented both groups, first as a player for the Red Bulls and later as a sporting director for New York City FC, spoke about the benefits of a wide-ranging network to *The Athletic*: 'It's a great sounding board for us to bounce ideas off and get feedback. From a scouting perspective, football strategy, sports science, medicine – we have the access to tap into all of that. Whether it's going there physically and visiting or reaching out on an email or the phone, my staff [at New York City FC] has the ability to do that and share information, which is really, really helpful.'

Now, Red Bull are at a crossroads and in a period of significant change. Rangnick's arrival altered the course of four clubs and he laid the foundations for them to build on in the future. He left his role in July 2020 after eight glorious years. Now, it remains to be seen how Red Bull do without him. The prediction is that they will continue in their rich vein: they have the fixed style of football, the money, the infrastructure and the player management system. Some changes to keep the machine running smoothly have already been made: Oliver Mintzlaff, previously the CEO of RB Leipzig, was moved to take over as the head of global soccer (a position he held previously in 2014 under the tutelage of Gérard Houllier), whilst the aforementioned adjustments such as Kevin Thelwell's arrival at the New York Red Bulls and the improved attention and investment in Red Bull Bragantino shows the company's commitment towards bettering their global empire.

Having been actively involved in football for over 15 years, Red Bull are entering a new era without their most significant figure. Whether they add a few new clubs to the umbrella or make more changes internally within their management remains to be seen, but a few things are certain: their presence in the football world will always be frowned upon no matter where they go and, despite that, they will continue to produce wonderful footballers and continue to play enthralling football.

CONTINUOUS IMPROVEMENT

A season-by-season review of how RB Leipzig
rose to challenge the Bundesliga's finest and make
their way into Europe's elite competition

KAIZEN, THE concept which refers to activities that continuously improve all functions and involve all members to achieve targets, can widely be associated with RB Leipzig in 2015. Following the departure of former coach Alexander Zorniger, who led 'Die Rotten Bullen' to the second division from 3. Liga, Ralf Rangnick, the man who had overseen this drastic improvement at the club, stepped in to complete the journey to the Bundesliga. Given the financial backing the club had, it was easy to predict that they would reach the German top flight in quick time. However, having spent a season in 2. Bundesliga where they missed out on the chance to earn promotion, it was clear the team lacked the maturity, the consistency and the right tactical outlook – Rangnick wanted to bring about that improvement over the course of the next year.

In Rangnick, the players were led by a man they could trust. After all, he was the one that had brought them to the club after careful evaluation and believed in their abilities. In addition to promotion, one of the aims of the season was to improve the quality of football on the pitch. Mainly, Rangnick wished for his team to be good on the ball in order to complement their high-pressing strategies, thus making the team more well-rounded. The start of the 2015/16 season included mixed results, such as a draw against Union Berlin, a loss to St Pauli and a win against Braunschweig, but this period of experimentation was part of the long-term learning curve that Leipzig were on. Having brought in some new names in Willi Orban, Stefan Ilsanker, Marcel Sabitzer and David Selke, helping them find their feet was going to take time.

Keeping the Rangnick philosophy of quick transitions and high pressure in mind, the manager tried out a variety of formations over the course of the season such as a 4-2-2-2, 4-2-3-1 and 4-1-3-2, with the aim of finding the right balance. It was the 4-2-2-2 that was the trusted set-up and, after a shaky start to the campaign, the team got into their stride and results came along to back that up. As Leipzig approached the winter, crucial wins over Nürnberg, Bochum and Arminia Bielefeld were recorded. The icing on the cake came just before the winter break. By defeating lowly FSV Frankfurt 3-1, Leipzig reached the top of the table in a convincing display of attacking football. A week later against Greuther Fürth, they conceded a late equaliser, only to score the winner in the dying seconds of the match – a testament to their mentality.

Vital to this run were players like Yussuf Poulsen. The Dane, by his own admission, isn't the most talented of footballers, but his strong mentality and intelligence made him a favourite of his manager. Sharing the attacking responsibilities with Selke, Poulsen's smart runs, ability to split defences and keep the opposition backline busy were useful characteristics for Leipzig. Another crucial player in this side was Sabitzer, who had just returned from a loan spell at Red Bull Salzburg. The Austrian's presence during the initial period of experimentation allowed Rangnick to find balance in the team. The former Rapid Wien player could play high up the pitch, behind the forwards or even deeper in midfield, connecting defence to attack. Having invested in his potential one year prior, the reward was finally there: he was becoming a mainstay in the first team.

Consisting of emerging talents like Orban, Emil Forsberg and Massimo Bruno, Leipzig looked good for the future. They had the youngest squad in the division, constantly fielding the youngest team each week and that made their achievements quite impressive. However, youthfulness, albeit positive in the long run, would create some trouble after the winter break. In complicated away trips – including against championship-chasing Freiburg – Leipzig lost without posing much of a threat and, as the season went on, the wear started to show. This was a scrappier part of the season, with the team stumbling as they approached the finish line and the ultimate goal.

The common belief in this division – one shared by Rangnick – is that two points per game on average is enough to confirm promotion, but Leipzig had a bit of trouble in this regard. They had to make their home a fortress, and hadn't dropped points at the Red Bull Arena since November 2015, and although things weren't all that positive towards the end, their strong earlier form was enough to see them through. On 8 May 2016, Forsberg, one of the league's best players, and Marcel Halstenberg, scored against Karlsruher to confirm promotion to the Bundesliga, finishing second behind Freiburg. Despite a tough end, Rangnick achieved what he had set out to do. He had a team tailored to his needs and improved them. Now, he left it to another man to carry on his good work.

TAKEAWAYS FROM THE SEASON

The youth-based approach was often problematic as the young players tired towards the end of the season and it showed in the results, but it was a good experience for the long run. After playing a lengthy season under pressure to finally reach the Bundesliga, there was plenty for the players to learn. The young group took the challenges of growing together as a team and developing individually very well. They managed to work their way out of problems, which provided a massive boost as they went into the top flight under a new manager. Rangnick's influence was vital and it was seen in the improvement of players such as Forsberg, Sabitzer and Poulsen.

In the Alps during the summer of 2013, a curious Ralph Hasenhüttl, equipped with a pair of binoculars and on a mountain bike, spied on training sessions conducted by Jürgen Klopp and Lucien Favre when they were at Borussia Dortmund and Borussia Mönchengladbach respectively, as they prepared for the season ahead. Having recently left VfR Aalen, who he had taken from the brink of relegation in the third tier to mid-table in the second division in under two years, the Austrian manager was eager to improve even further. Picking up some points from two of the brightest managers in Germany was a good way to start, and just a few months later in October 2013, those learnings would be put to the test when he was given the reins at FC Ingolstadt, who were sitting at the bottom of 2. Bundesliga.

Once again, Hasenhüttl would weave his magic. By the summer of 2015, Ingolstadt were preparing for their first season in the Bundesliga, and the manager's stock was quickly rising. As a forward in his playing days, Hasenhüttl didn't have the shiniest of reputations, playing mainly in his home country, including a spell at Austria Salzburg pre-Red Bull, and briefly with Bayern Munich's second team.

His wife, Sandra, often used to say that her husband would make a better coach than player – and she was right. He was a fighter. At Aalen, Hasenhüttl was diagnosed with a strain of potentially fatal hantavirus. He was weakened but beat the disease and took Aalen upwards. At Ingolstadt, he took over an average squad and made them second division champions against all odds. In the Bundesliga, his and his team's impact was so great that even Pep Guardiola was wowed. When his Bayern team beat Ingolstadt at the Allianz Arena, the Spaniard remarked: 'Today we encountered the best team we've been up against so far this season.'

It was in the Alps where Hasenhüttl's next journey was being considered. He met Rangnick at a restaurant to discuss a move to Leipzig ahead of their likely promotion to the top flight. A deal was agreed. In the reverse fixture against Guardiola's Bayern, Hasenhüttl took charge of his final game at the Audi Sportpark. A win for the Bavarians saw them clinch the title, and while on one end they were jubilant, on the other, there were tears. A beautiful journey had just come to an end. Hasenhüttl had spurred the club on to survive in the league for another season, but he was going elsewhere.

Often compared to Klopp for their career paths and similar playing styles, Hasenhüttl is actually quite the opposite. With some of the Austrian manager's passions being the piano and tennis, two activities which require patience, it comes as no surprise that Hasenhüttl is always so calm and composed on the touchline. His man-management is excellent, and he does his best to maintain strong relationships with his players. Early in the 2016/17 season at the Red Bull Arena, he dropped Forsberg despite the player's gleaming reputation, stating that the Swede lacked fitness. The tough love paid off. Soon, Forsberg was back and once again was at his best, this time in a much tougher division. Discipline is imperative for the manager – something exemplified by his daily 7am yoga sessions before work. At Leipzig, he and Rangnick saw eye to eye on several matters.

A purveyor of winning the ball high up the pitch, creating width from the full-backs and pure high-intensity football, Hasenhüttl's version of the 4-2-2-2 was unlike the style he used at his previous two clubs, but the talent he had at his disposal and Rangnick's emphasis meant it could easily be deployed at Leipzig. In this versatile set-up, the attacking midfielders, usually Sabitzer and Forsberg, would create space with their shrewd, inward movement while the full-backs were supportive in their attacking zones. Diego Demme was important. The defensive midfielder's work rate and excellent vision could help free up the players in front of him, giving Leipzig a fluent attacking approach. His talents also allowed Naby Keïta, who had just joined the club from Red Bull Salzburg, to shine. With Demme in the side, Leipzig would often evolve to a 4-2-4 while on the ball as the German's presence created a solid backline.

He told *Football Paradise* that his team always aimed to get better at four aspects: pressing, ball possession, positioning and what to do when they lost the ball. 'Every opposition needs to be played in a different way and the formation depends on the opposition's strengths. But we trained [mostly] with 4-2-2-2, 4-4-3 and 3-4-3 because we could adapt that for most games,' he said. 'Leipzig playing against the ball is famous because of the perfect symmetry in their rows. It is a very intensive way to defend because we have a very high number of players to attack the ball, and [when they win the ball from the opposition] the whole team has to be prepared in where they have to be and how to attack. The team has to be perfectly aligned. The distance between the single players should create triangles and all across the pitch they have the option to pick and choose from these three angles to maybe force the opponent to lose the ball. To learn this takes a lot of automatism and [this] requires the most amount of time in training.'

In terms of results, one of the most significant came in Leipzig's first home game against Dortmund. Keïta scored an 89th-minute winner to set Hasenhüttl off on a Klopp-like enthusiastic 50-yard sprint. Over the summer, the squad added more depth, bringing in more young talent. Dayot Upamecano, Oliver Burke and, most significantly, Timo Werner signed up. Expectations were low, but the sky was the limit for Leizpig. 'Die Rotten Bullen' won ten and drew three of their first 13 matches – the longest undefeated streak for a promoted team in Bundesliga history – finding themselves in an unanticipated title fight with Carlo Ancelotti's Bayern.

Coincidentally, Ingolstadt were the first to claim a win over Leipzig that season, and just 11 days after that, a first-half blitz saw Bayern claim a 3-0 win over them. This controversial seven-year-old club had just spent the first half of the season overcoming the giants of German football. Schalke, Hamburg, Bayer Leverkusen and Hertha Berlin had all been credibly beaten. Just like in the previous campaign, the second half was underwhelming, albeit on a lesser scale, explained best by a 3-0 home defeat to struggling Hamburg, where Leipzig, and especially Upamecano's poor defensive shape and lack of aerial prowess were exposed. Luck was on their side, however, as Dortmund's inconsistency meant that Leipzig didn't suffer too much in the table. Factor in Werner's incredible 21-goal debut season, and there was enough to be satisfied with.

By the end, Leipzig qualified for the Champions League – something the management didn't see coming at the start of the season. In their final home game against champions Bayern, they squared off for one of the best matches in Bundesliga history. Having led 4-2 with minutes to play, Robert Lewandowski scored in the 84th minute to raise the tension, and then Bayern produced another onslaught. One minute into stoppage time, David Alaba scored a stunning free kick and, soon after, Arjen Robben went on a trademark run and finish to seal a wild 5-4 away victory. The result was a blot on a successful season, with the club finishing second.

On several occasions during the campaign, Hasenhüttl had experimented with various styles, such as the 4-3-3, and had put more emphasis on possession – this was part of the club and team's learning curve. After an enjoyable debut campaign in the Bundesliga, Leipzig could now look forward to Europe's premier club cup competition.

TAKEAWAYS FROM THE SEASON

RB Leipzig's first season in the top flight was full of positives and Hasenhüttl was most certainly the right man to take the club forward.

The players dealt with pressure well and made full use of their abilities. Their success was fully deserved as the Austrian manager's decision-making and adjustments throughout the season were in the best interests of the team. Leipzig scored the most goals from counter-attacks (11) – proof of their speed and efficiency – whilst their improved maturity to hold on to results was a plus. In sticking with their idea of mainly using younger players, the squad had a real desire to succeed at the highest level and achieved the best result for a promoted side since Kaiserslautern, who won the Meisterschale in the 1997/98 season.

At the Champions League draw in Nyon, Switzerland, Leipzig, in Pot 4, got a favourable result. Facing the possibility of being paired against some of Europe's finest, they got a depleted Monaco, who had lost their Ligue 1-winning stars Kylian Mbappé, Bernardo Silva and Tiémoué Bakayoko, along with Beşiktaş and Porto. By December, Leipzig were left disappointed. Their European ambition was in tatters and expectations from their debut Champions League campaign were miles off what transpired on the pitch. A win and a draw against Monaco, two losses to Beşiktaş and a win and loss against Porto meant that they finished third in their group with seven points and were demoted to the Europa League.

Leipzig certainly didn't have a bad team, and it wouldn't be too controversial to suggest that they were arguably better than their competitors in that group. What made the difference was a variety of factors. Firstly, 2017/18 was a season unlike any other in the club's history. It was a campaign that included several *Englische Wocken*, English weeks, a term used to describe a period of matches where teams play midweek fixtures – as is the norm in England. The team lacked the ability to compete on three different fronts. Over the course of the season, important players got injured, leaving the remaining squad with a dysfunctional team to play with. Forsberg, Halstenberg and Sabitzer suffered long-term lay-offs and the grind of playing two, sometimes three games in the space of seven days was showing. This was an unconventional but important experience for the club as a whole.

Another noteworthy factor was Hasenhüttl's switching of styles. Throughout the season, the manager tried a variety of formations, line-ups and tactical implementations. Apart from the primary 4-2-2-2, there was also a 3-4-3, 4-4-2 and a 4-3-3 frequently used. Hasenhüttl's desire to move to a possession-based style of play didn't work out well. The players weren't best equipped to master the possession game: having security on the ball and maintaining their dominance in the opposition half was a tough challenge and, as they were playing some matches under pressure to perhaps better the previous season, this created complex problems. Although it worked when the schedule was favourable, in the long run it wasn't suitable.

The first half of the season featured some fine results, despite the busy schedule. Most famously, Dortmund's struggles against Leipzig continued, this time losing 3-2 at the Westfalenstadion. However, inconsistency over the winter break led to a drop down the table. A 4-0 loss to Hoffenheim followed by a 3-2 home defeat to Hertha saw them outside the Champions League places.

In the Europa League, it could be said that Leipzig took their foot off the gas to focus on their domestic season. After beating Napoli and Zenit St Petersburg in two difficult rounds, they fell to eventual runners-up Marseille. Results in the league slightly improved after that elimination, including a 1-1 draw against Dortmund and a 2-1 win over Bayern, arguably the most famous result in their history, but the damage from the first half of the season was clear and the results towards the end of this campaign ended Leipzig's hopes of returning to the Champions League. A four-week period in April saw heavy defeats to Leverkusen (1-4), Hoffenheim (2-5) and Mainz (3-0) as well as a draw against Werder Bremen. Leipzig finished sixth and qualified for the Europa League.

It's worth reiterating that this wasn't a terrible season. The club were growing faster than expected and making Europe twice in two seasons immediately after promotion was an achievement. Over the course of the campaign, players like Sabitzer, Forsberg and Halstenberg committed their future to the club. These were players who were on the rise from the lower divisions and were now playing Continental football as well as representing their respective national teams – Leipzig recognised their worth and rapid growth.

TAKEAWAYS FROM THE SEASON

A season of missed opportunities, rather than one of failure: it was clear from the 2017/18 season that RB Leipzig were not equipped for two games in a week in two high-level competitions. The team was lacking defensively and Hasenhüttl's constant switching of formations plus his experimentation were not working out. The players started to tire towards the end of the campaign, losing crucial matches and, given the Austrian manager's insistence on using a core group of players, the squad was stretched. Considering 'Die Rotten Bullen' were growing far more quickly than they expected, they had a lot to fix if they were to continue in this vein of being one of the Bundesliga's best clubs.

For the latter half of the 2017/18 campaign, Hasenhüttl's future had been a major talking point. There were rumours of him being offered a new deal, with Rangnick even mentioning at a press conference that the coach would be given an extension, but nothing materialised. When the summer came around, the Austrian was gone, with the belief that the deal he was offered was not long enough. He ended his existing contract a year earlier than expected and Leipzig went after Julian Nagelsmann for the 2019/20 season. In the meantime, Rangnick would once again take on the double role of sporting director and head coach as Leipzig entered a transition season, hoping to amend the few wrongs of the previous months. The aim was simple: bring back the Red Bull DNA.

Too much of the previous campaign had been spent trying to switch to a possession-based game. Under Rangnick, Leipzig continued to show flexibility in formations, but the style of play returned to their famed intense pressing high up the pitch and breaking on the counter. The changes were there to see in the statistics. In the league, Leipzig's average possession numbers dropped to 50 per cent from 54 per cent as the team's pragmatism, desire to work without the ball and ability to effectively switch play were improved. Rangnick tried the 4-2-2-2, the most preferred, along with the occasional 5-3-2. The team behind the team had a huge hand in this. Jesse Marsch and Robert Klauß, his two assistants, as well as Lars Kornetka, the video analyst, were central to these changes. Kornetka was a vital figure who identified his own team's strengths and weaknesses, as well as analysing opponents – his insight was valued greatly.

Right from the off, it was easy to see that the focus was on the Bundesliga and returning to the Champions League. Drawn against Red Bull Salzburg, Celtic and Rosenborg in the Europa League, Rangnick fielded some of his fringe players in the competition, such as Matheus Cunha, Bruma and Yvon Mvogo. Although this would've been a good chance for the club to stamp their authority in Europe, the coach saw more benefit in the domestic competitions. An insipid start to the season included a 4-1 defeat to Dortmund and a home draw against Fortuna Düsseldorf. Leipzig were still undeterred, believing that the loss in Dortmund was unlucky and in the next few fixtures, they showed their class. By winning games that they were largely expected to win – including a 6-0 thumping of Nürnberg – they climbed up the table.

What was most rewarding about their improved form was the fact that they were defensively astute. Two successive 3-0 wins over Hertha and Leverkusen proved just that. The win at the Olympiastadion was one of their most impressive of the season – a complete team performance bagged a deserved result. As fixtures came in thick and fast across three competitions in the winter period, inconsistency followed, but after a 2-1 home defeat against Dortmund, Leipzig were unbeaten until the very last day of the league. A dominant period of successive wins between March and April 2019 showed just how well this team was improving. Coming up against solid opposition in Schalke, Hertha, Leverkusen, Wolfsburg, Mönchengladbach and Freiburg, Leipzig were dominant and confirmed their return to the Champions League in wonderful fashion.

They conceded the fewest goals in the league, 29, with players like Ibrahima Konaté and Péter Gulácsi coming to the fore. Despite losing Keïta earlier in the season, Leipzig promoted from within, giving opportunities to Konrad Laimer. Additionally, holding on to sought-after Werner was important. Once again, he was the team's top scorer.

There was a chance to win silverware at the end of the season. In the DFB-Pokal, having swept through the opposition, they faced record cup winners Bayern in a bid to win their first cup. However, Leipzig came up against an inspired Manuel Neuer in Berlin. Despite a strong showing for over an hour, the Bavarian outfit's know-how came in handy. Lewandowski's brace was added to by a fine Kingsley Coman strike and sealed a 3-0 win, leaving Leipzig with a sour feeling.

Regardless of that, it was a season beyond their expectations. Third in the league and cup finalists was something for Nagelsmann to build on. Focusing on settling the squad and their playing philosophy, the team gained confidence as the season progressed and it was something the young players needed. The transition season was an immense success.

TAKEAWAYS FROM THE SEASON

There is a strong loyalty and trust towards Rangnick, not only from his players, but from his employers as well and Leipzig reaped the rewards of this good relationship. After a stuttering 2017/18 campaign, getting back the Red Bull DNA of high pressing and intensity was crucial, and more importantly, becoming a defensively sound team was necessary. Leipzig conceded 27 fewer goals than the previous season (75 in 2017/18 and 48 in 2018/19) and Rangnick left a solid foundation for Nagelsmann. A much-needed efficient season on all fronts.

In this period, RB Leipzig also formed their women's team, starting in the 2016/17 season. RB Frauen absorbed the playing squad of FFV Leipzig and had a squad of professionals. They began in the Landesliga, the sixth tier, and attracted the anger of their rivals for the way they got a free pass to this level, rather than starting right at the bottom. Since then, they have made their way up the divisions. As of August 2020, they are set to play 2. Frauen-Bundesliga, the second division. Similar to the men's team, they rose through the ranks with a youth-centred approach, although they do have a financial advantage over many other clubs. They are expected to challenge Wolfsburg's dominance on the women's football scene in Germany over the next few years.

BACKLASH

'FOR ME, as a fan of Chemie Leipzig, it's important to emphasise that we stand for the opposite of what RB Leipzig embodies. Chemie is a club that is supported and run by fans. Ultras and fan clubs have an institutional say in all important decisions. They support match operations, which would be impossible for the club without volunteers in the areas of media relations, stewardship and ticket sales,' says Bastian Pauly, a Chemie supporter since 1997 and member since 2008. He adds: 'Chemie cultivates a very romantic image of football. In the Alfred-Kunze-Sportpark in Leutzscher (the home ground of Chemie Leipzig) you can see, smell and feel what has made the club so great for over 100 years. This positive awareness of tradition is a unique selling point that is becoming more and more important for more and more fans. The number of members and stadium spectators has grown constantly in recent years – despite or perhaps because of Red Bull.'

Those thoughts are echoed by Matthias Löffler, a Lokomotive Leipzig season ticket holder since 2004 and co-author of *50 Jahre 1. FC Lokomotive Leipzig – Die Chronik in Bildern* (50 Years of Lokomotive Leipzig – The Chronicle in Pictures): 'In terms of Lok fans, I would say most of us tend to ignore them [RB Leipzig] (which is also my approach), but they got more annoying over the years. There is no rivalry between

Lok and RB Leipzig. There can't be. Even if some people try to make it one there will always be only one derby in the city: Lok versus Chemie. But of course, some of the Lok fans see them as the "enemy".'

Löffler continues: 'The proper football fans should concentrate on their own clubs. Promote them, help them, work passionately for them. I've spoken to a few people over the years at Lok who have said to me: "When I was new in Leipzig, I went to see a couple of RB Leipzig games. Through a friend (or sometimes by accident) I later came here and witnessed a Lok game. That was great. Real football. The fans suffered, cheered and really experienced the game. That's why Lok is my team now." I like that. For me it's about those three or four people and not the thousands who want to see [games against] Bayern once in a while. I am very positive that tradition is also something for the future. How disconnected are top-flight football clubs from the fans nowadays?'

For decades, both Chemie and Lokomotive Leipzig have despised each other. They're eternal rivals, detesting everything about the other and have a distinct legacy in German football. Both clubs were created by the Communist state – Chemie in 1963 and Lok in 1966 – from the foundations of other clubs. While the former embraced its left and anti-fascist ideology, the latter has mostly been on the opposite end of the political spectrum, which often leads to extremism. Despite the hatred these two share, they can easily agree on one aspect: their disapproval of RB Leipzig.

As Pauly and Löffler point out, RB Leipzig feels artificial, something that isn't theirs and something they can never accept. Chemie and Lok embody the city, as represented by their colours: the green and white of Chemie signifies their state, Saxony, where Leipzig is based; the blue and yellow of Lok signifies Leipzig; while the red and white of RB signifies Red Bull, the Austrian energy drink. From there stems the disdain.

Just like the pair in Leipzig, much of Germany has followed in their dislike of RB Leipzig and Red Bull in general. From the club's first game in the fifth-tier Oberliga against Carl Zeiss Jena, right until the present day in the Bundesliga, the club have faced backlash from opposition fans and are the country's most hated football club. German football is well known for its fan welfare, the protection of clubs from over-commercialisation and, of course, the famous 50 + 1 rule. Taking the other route from these factors was always bound to attract intense animosity.

As RB Leipzig made their way through Germany's league ladder, several of the country's most passionate sets of fans made their voices heard. At Hallescher FC, when RB Leipzig were in the third division, fans pelted stones at the team bus and donned T-shirts which read *Tradition Hat Einen Namen* (tradition has a name). Later against Hansa Rostock, fans refused to enter the stadium for the first ten minutes of their match.

Leipzig's rise has been met with incredible rage – clubs that have had local rivals for decades hate the Red Bull-backed club more and that scrutiny only rose as they made their way through to 2. Bundesliga, where some of Germany's most traditional clubs play. Before they even kicked a ball in the second division, rival fans had already planned protests, and fan groups from ten clubs even launched the *'Nein zu RB'* (no to Red Bull) campaign.

Union Berlin, an example of the country's fervent fan culture, were silently vocal in their disapproval of Leipzig when they visited the Stadion An der Alten Försterei in September 2014. The 20,000 fans were silent for the first 15 minutes of the league game and, with permission from the Union management, the supporters, clad entirely in black, handed out pamphlets which read 'Football culture is dying in Leipzig – Union is alive' along with a few paragraphs explaining why Leipzig were everything wrong with modern football. A season later, they replaced the traditional opposition profile in their matchday programme with details on bull farming.

Just over five years later, in January 2020, when Union were in the Bundesliga and marching to the Red Bull Arena from the train station, the fans were at it again: they dressed in black, carrying flags, a coffin and funeral crosses that bore words such as 'emotion', 'tradition' and '*fankultur*', led by a massive banner with the motto '*In Leipzig Stirbt der Fußball*' (football dies in Leipzig).

More protests had come from some of Germany's oldest and most traditional clubs in 2. Bundesliga. Against Heidenheim, supporters pelted the Leipzig team bus with fake dollar bills that had a picture of Dietrich Mateschitz printed on them, along with the text '*Scheiß Red Bull*' (shitty Red Bull). Away at Karlsruher in 2015, many Leipzig supporters received letters not to travel to the game, or they would face violence. Clearly, there was no place in German football for Mateschitz or his world-famous company.

With their subsequent promotion to the top flight, the tension only continued to grow. In the first round of the 2016/17 DFB Pokal, 'Die Rotten Bullen' squared off against Dynamo Dresden away from home in what turned out to be a grossly symbolic match in the club's young history. Dynamo, known for their extreme ways, hadn't been afraid to voice their concerns over matters in German football in recent times. Previous years had seen them earn a suspension from the cup for crowd trouble, and they were risking the wrath of the authorities once again when they came up against Leipzig. Their fans unfurled offensive banners, hit a Leipzig player on the head with a coin and, most disgustingly, threw a severed bull's head near the pitch. Their protest saw them receive a €60,000 fine and a partial stadium closure, but more importantly to the fans, they had made their message clear.

A few weeks later in RB Leipzig's Bundesliga debut away against Hoffenheim, the opposition fans sarcastically displayed placards stating they wanted their title as Germany's most hated club back. Hoffenheim, whose rise to the top flight was bankrolled by controversial billionaire software entrepreneur Dietmar Hopp, had faced a similar backlash for several years before becoming a mainstay in the Bundesliga. Germany's conservative fans had no room for these two – they needed traditional names such as Kaiserslautern, Saarbrücken and Uerdingen, amongst others – clubs that had earned their fame on the pitch.

Against FC Köln in September 2016, the fans blocked the street that led to the Müngersdorfer Stadion and prevented the Leipzig team bus from entering. This peaceful protest resulted in a 15-minute delay to kick-off. More comically, Köln wore one-off shirts for that specific game. Their shirt sponsor, REWE, the supermarket chain based in the city, customised the shirts, replacing their own logo with the branding of their own Maximal G energy drink in what was playfully dubbed as the 'battle of the energy drinks' by the club's English Twitter account.

Borussia Dortmund, one of Germany's most vocal and fan-centred clubs, have been loud in this regard as well. When they were scheduled to visit the Red Bull Arena in 2016 for their first away game that season, thousands of their ultras refused to make the trip, instead choosing to watch their youth team at their old ground, Stadion Rote Erde, whilst following the senior team's progress over the radio. The club's CEO, Hans-Joachim Watzke, was a stark critic of Leipzig from the start – even when they were playing in the second division: 'They do very good work in sport. But it's a club built to push up the revenues of Red Bull, and nothing else … Leipzig, from an economic perspective, they have the most money behind Bayern Munich in Germany because they have Red Bull behind them. And if they want to, they can pay any price. It's good for the league [that Leipzig are amongst the top] because the race to be champions was closed, but the construct of Leipzig is not for me. In German football, the clubs belong to the fans, to the spectators.'

Ahead of the return fixture at the Westfalenstadion in February 2017, matters got ugly in a shameful scene for German football. Nearly 400 Dortmund ultras gathered outside the stadium to block the Leipzig team bus from reaching the ground but after those attempts failed, the ultras turned their attention to the arriving Leipzig fans. Soon, violence broke out with the Dortmund group hurling stones, cans and beer cases whilst also throwing lit fireworks at them. Police intervened, using batons and pepper spray, with four officers and a dog suffering injury. By the end, the authorities filed 28 charges for breaches of law concerning explosives, assault and dangerous bodily injury as 'Die Borussen' were disgraced by their loyal fans. On the pitch, Dortmund won but they suffered a moral defeat due to the actions of the fans – even in the stands, offensive banners were aimed at Leipzig and Ralf Rangnick. In the aftermath, both clubs released statements condemning the actions, whilst Watzke revealed he had received death threats.

In the years that followed, clubs have continued with their protests against RB Leipzig, albeit in a more sensible and peaceful manner. The ultras from Bayern Munich, Borussia Dortmund and Köln have boycotted every away game against Leipzig since their promotion, whilst Freiburg's active fan scene hosts meetings to discuss the issue. Silent protests such as those by Borussia Mönchengladbach for 19 minutes in 2016, to represent their founding year, 1900, have continued whilst banners like Bayern's infamous 'Fuck RB', unfurled away at the Red Bull Arena and at home in 2019 and 2020 are still prevalent.

Freiburg, who have become a sustainable Bundesliga outfit in recent times, took aim at the club and the growing commercialisation in German football when it was announced in April 2020 that the league would be one of the first to resume, but only behind closed doors, after the COVID-19 pandemic halted sport across the world. Disappointed that the DFL (Deutsche Fußball Liga) was putting money ahead of health, two ultras groups said in a statement: 'The hypocrisy disgusts us. You call that humility? Without continuous commercialisation, we wouldn't be in this predicament. You wouldn't be reliant on TV money to pay seven-figure salaries and service debts, and we wouldn't have to watch a game against a soulless company team that only exists because of these very developments. Football must change radically.'

In the media, outlets such as *Bild*, *Sport Bild*, *Kicker* and *Sky Deutschland*, amongst others, have continued with their code of ethics and professionalism by talking about the club as they would do for anyone else. They tend to keep discussions solely about the team's excellent football rather than matters off the pitch.

However, *11Freunde* is the biggest and only mainstream media outlet to consistently criticise and question RB Leipzig. In 2020, ahead of the top-of-the-table clash between Bayern and Leipzig, they published a statement on their website saying they would not cover the game live as they wished to distance themselves from the media's normalisation of the club as well as Red Bull: 'We decided against it anyway [covering the match]. It is not because we don't care about click numbers and don't need people to read our content. We decided against it – once again – because we do not want to normalise the construct of RB Leipzig any further. Which is why we have never reported about Leipzig in the printed magazine or on 11freunde.de in the conventional sense.' They did the same a few months later when RB Leipzig reached the semi-finals of the Champions League.

Similarly, a group of Leipzig natives started producing a blog, *Zwangsbeglüeckt*, which translates to 'positively happy'. The name was born from a statement by Dietrich Mateschitz when he threatened the DFL after RB Leipzig were going through licensing issues after promotion from the third division. The Austrian entrepreneur said: 'Allow me to be frank. We don't want to make anyone happy, and frankly, we don't need that.' The blog criticises RB Leipzig and their presence in modern German football.

With the entire country against them, it's only natural that Leipzig acknowledge the negativity they face. And yet, they are unbothered by it and undeterred in their objectives. Rangnick spoke to *DW* about it: 'As far as I can see there are many clubs in the Bundesliga that have no problem with how we have built up the club. In eastern Germany, we are the third most popular club in the league. I think there are fewer "RB haters" than there were during our time in the second division. We are very happy with our sponsor, but we never think for one minute about how we can sell more cans [of Red Bull]. What drives and motivates us is developing players. We are not a marketing tool.'

The club's former CEO and current head of global soccer for Red Bull, Oliver Mintzlaff, spoke about how Leipzig provided a different element of improved competition in the Bundesliga. Talking to the *New York Times* in 2016, he said: 'I was on a plane with Karl-Heinz Rummenigge, the chief executive of Bayern Munich ... He said, and I agree entirely, that it would be awesome for Bayern to have more competition. The secret of the Premier League is that there are five or six strong teams. Here, it is just Bayern and Dortmund. We need more. It is about having a competitive league, not just one club that wins every year. With the power of Red Bull and a lot of hard work, in a few years, we could help that.'

Bizarrely, there has also been criticism of the club from its own fans. While Red Bull brought along changes in the football and infrastructure, they left some of the supporters behind, leading to disputes between groups. In December 2018, prior to a match between Roter Stern Leipzig and RB Leipzig II in the women's division, supporters of both teams set off multicoloured smoke bombs, raising awareness against discrimination and revealing a banner that read 'love football, hate sexism'. The organisers of this act, the Red Aces ultras group and Fraktion Red Pride, then received letters from the club which banned them from games, in a move that angered the club's other supporters. Soon, there was an issue with the use of pyrotechnics at the club's senior men's games after the management took a dislike to their use during the 2018/19 season.

German fan culture is extremely political, with supporters using their platform to raise their voice against social injustices, with the aim of seeing changes, and pyrotechnics are an imperative supplement to that. The two instances above were coupled with Mintzlaff's enraging comments: 'We want peaceful football here. We want fans from Leipzig and the surrounding areas to be able to travel to games in safety and we don't want pyrotechnics … We stand for certain fundamental values, including anti-racism and anti-discrimination, and that is not going to change. But we don't see ourselves as a platform for political messages, whatever they may be.'

Disappointed with the club's stance, fan groups got together with a statement of their own, along with a banner during a game against Eintracht Frankfurt in February 2019 that read *'Wer viel verspricht, vergisst auch viel – wir müssen reden – dialog jetzt!'* (those who promise now also forget a lot – we need to talk – dialogue now!). 'What exactly is going wrong at our club?' said the statement by the Leipzig fans, who also organised the banner. 'We don't feel respected as fans and we don't feel taken seriously. We're used to that in other stadiums across the country but in our own stadium, we won't allow ourselves to be treated as the opinionless, conformist consumers that other fan scenes accuse us of being.'

Earlier in 2017 after Mateschitz had criticised the German government's decision to open borders for refugees from the war in Syria, the fans voiced their disgust. The Red Bull supremo was present at a home game against Schalke that year and the fans revealed a banner that read: 'The patron of the most authoritarian club calls himself a pluralist. What a joke.' *Servus TV*, an Austrian-based channel owned by the Red Bull

Media House has attracted criticism as well as they've offered a platform to many far-right activists.

In March 2020, the Red Aces, one of the most popular groups at the club who were behind many movements, announced their dissolution with a simple message and no explanation: 'Nine years of utopia. Nine years of change. Fought against resistance, endured it, sometimes won, often lost. Always looking for a place for our ideals. This path is now coming to an end. Reached for the stars, saw them, but never reached them.' Leipzig were internally adding to their lack of popularity. Another outspoken fan group is Rasenballisten, who, in their words, stand for the team and not the club. Their website makes it clear by saying they're fully supportive of football, the city, the fan culture, but not the sponsors. An anonymous member of Rasenballisten said to *DW*: 'It's not a secret that Mateschitz's worldview is populist, some would even say racist,' as he explained the group is against the views of the Red Bull owner.

In a country fighting to carry tradition into the future, there are plenty of people that don't want to see the club succeed. Uli Hesse, the author of *Tor!: The Story of German Football* and one of the members of the editorial staff at *11Freunde* said to me: 'I respect the club on a purely professional, footballing level, but I think they should not be allowed to play in the Bundesliga. They are clearly breaking the spirit of the law, meaning the 50 + 1 rule, and perhaps even the letter of the law. They have changed German football by setting a dangerous precedent. Dangerous for our football culture, I mean, not necessarily for the game as such.'

He continued: 'RB Leipzig's success will certainly help their acceptance among the more casual supporters and the public in general. The first half of the 2019/20 season was a good case in point, because you'd often hear people – fans and journalists – remark on the fact that Leipzig were making the league more interesting. I'd reckon that about two thirds of

German football fans will say: "Wouldn't it be great if, finally, a team other than Bayern wins the Bundesliga?" And one third will say: "I'd rather have Bayern win in all eternity than see Leipzig lift the title.'"

His thoughts are shared by commentator Derek Rae, who has covered German football professionally since 2010, having followed the league for decades prior: 'Their success will be a hard one to swallow for fans of clubs who have done it a different way. But I do agree there is an inevitability about it so I don't think it will take anyone particularly by surprise. The 50 + 1 rule is under threat without doubt.'

A Bundesliga or DFB Pokal title is almost inevitable soon, but RB Leipzig, no matter how popular or successful they become in the coming years, may never be accepted amongst the German football faithful.

THE BATTLE WITHIN

THE GRIMALDI Forum, Monaco, 31 August 2018. It's the Europa League draw ahead of the 2018/19 season. Hernán Crespo, a winner of the competition in 1999 with Parma and a guest assisting at the event, picks the ball for Red Bull Salzburg, or FC Salzburg, as they're known in European competitions, from Pot 1. A few minutes later, he moves on to Pot 3 and draws RB Leipzig for the same group – a clash that was written in the stars. Joining them would be Scottish and Norwegian champions Celtic and Rosenborg respectively in what was a competitive quartet. At a draw that created some exciting fixtures, Group B was one of the major talking points of the day.

The two sister clubs meeting in European competition had been a much-debated, and for the neutral, a much-awaited contest. Many believed that it would test the integrity of the game and put UEFA's regulations in a tight spot. Ever since Leipzig's surprise second-place finish and subsequent qualification for the Champions League in 2017, this topic has been in the spotlight. Since Leipzig qualified for European competition, Red Bull have been adamant that they are merely a sponsor of Salzburg, with their main focus being their ownership of Leipzig, although most fans aren't buying it.

Leipzig's entry into the Champions League ahead of the 2017/18 campaign was put into doubt as UEFA regulations stated that no 'individual or entity' can have a 'decisive influence over the activities of more than one club in its tournaments'. Article 5, Integrity of the Competition, states that the team that finishes higher in its domestic league would earn a place in the Champions League. This meant that if UEFA had found the article being breached, Salzburg, the Austrian champions in 2017, would've got that place and Leipzig would've been barred from Europe altogether – not even getting the chance to play in the Europa League, seeing as teams have a possibility of dropping down after exiting the Champions League.

European football's governing body has handled such cases in the past. In 1997, Greek side AEK Athens weren't allowed to play in the UEFA Cup because their owner, ENIC, the investment group, also owned Czech side Slavia Prague. Four years later, Swiss outfit Servette dropped out of the same competition to allow Paris Saint-Germain to play in it. Both clubs were backed by French television conglomerate, Canal+. Fast forward 16 years and the same problem arose again. The similarities between Salzburg and Leipzig were clear to see: both donned the same colours, their crests were identical, they both play at the Red Bull Arena in their respective cities and they have shared several players in the past. Controversially, UEFA did not see it that way.

On 20 June 2017, UEFA confirmed that Article 5 of the Champions League's regulations had not been breached and both Salzburg and Leipzig would be allowed to compete on the Continental stage: 'Following a thorough investigation, and further to several important governance and structural changes made by the clubs (regarding corporate matters, financing, personnel, sponsorship arrangements, etc.), the Club Financial Control Body deemed that no individual or legal entity had anymore a decisive influence over more than one club participating in a UEFA club competition.' The structural changes mentioned in that statement included many people in management positions at Salzburg leaving their role, while

Oliver Mintzlaff, Red Bull's head of global soccer and Ralf Rangnick, the technical director for all clubs under the Red Bull umbrella, committed themselves fully to Leipzig in the months leading up to UEFA's decision.

In the Champions League that season, Leipzig were drawn against Monaco, Porto and Beşiktaş, while Salzburg once again failed to make the group stage, falling to Croatia's Rijeka in the third qualifying round. The Austrians did go through to the Europa League and won a group consisting of Marseille, Konyaspor and Vitória. As they reached the knockout rounds, the possibility of them facing Leipzig came about once again – the Germans finished third in their group in Europe's premier competition, dropping down to the secondary tournament. They avoided each other in the round of 32: Leipzig played Napoli and won; Salzburg toppled Real Sociedad. In the following round, they were kept apart again: Leipzig overcame Zenit St Petersburg; Salzburg shocked Borussia Dortmund. In the quarter-finals, when a clash seemed most likely, Leipzig drew and fell to Marseille, Salzburg dramatically beat Lazio, before losing to the French side in the last four.

The pair meeting in an official competition for the first time was inevitable and in the following season, when Leipzig qualified for the Europa League and Salzburg once again failed to qualify for the Champions League competition proper, Crespo drew them together in the same group. The reaction was exactly as expected. UEFA competition director Giorgio Marchetti had to reiterate that both clubs were separate entities and that there was no issue with them playing each other. Social media was abuzz, claiming the duel between the two to be the Red Bull derby. In Leipzig, Rangnick was happy with the result of the draw, telling the fans to expect an enthralling fixture, while on the Salzburg end, coach Marco Rose and sporting director Christoph Freund spoke highly about the common style of football the two teams play. Dietrich Mateschitz, the mastermind behind this all, was pleased: 'May the better team win. It's a great story for everyone in our family and it will be interesting and fun.'

On the first matchday of the campaign, Salzburg travelled to Germany for the clash and Rose's team sent out a strong XI to contest the fixture:

[4-3-1-2] Walke – Lainer, Ramalho, Pongračić, Ulmer (C) – Haidara, Samassékou, Schlager – Wolf – Dabbur, Yabo
Substitutes: Stanković, Todorović, Onguene, Mwepu, Junzović, Minamino, Gulbrandsen

In the opposition dugout, Rangnick chose to rest some of his best players, opting to keep the team fresh for a difficult away trip to Eintracht Frankfurt at the weekend:

[4-2-3-1] Mvogo – Laimer, Upamecano, Konaté, Mukiele – Kampl (C), Ilsanker – Sabitzer, Cunha, Bruma – Augustin
Substitutes: Gulácsi, Halstenberg, Orban, Majetschak, Demme, Forsberg, Poulsen

In Konrad Laimer, Dayot Upamecano, Kevin Kampl, Stefan Ilsanker and Marcel Sabitzer, Leipzig had five former Salzburg players starting for them. As both clubs claimed when the draw was made, the match was played with professionalism, with both teams putting corporate structures to the side and focusing entirely on what happened on the pitch.

In the first battle between the two sister clubs, it was the older that drew first blood. Moanes Dabbur took advantage of a misguided back pass by Ilsanker and despite, Yvon Mvogo's best efforts, the Israeli forward found the back of the net. Just two minutes later, the Austrians were at it again. More bad defending from Leipzig left a gap for Salzburg to exploit and allowed captain Andreas Ulmer to run through and set up Amadou Haidara for the simplest of finishes. The Malian midfielder was a star on the pitch, controlling play and spurring his team on. Salzburg went into the break with a surprise 2-0 lead, but Leipzig didn't back down.

Rangnick used all his three substitutes at half-time, taking off Nordi Mukiele, Bruma and Jean-Kévin Augustin for the more experienced Marcel Halstenberg, Diego Demme and Yussuf Poulsen, and the response came. Twenty minutes from time, Laimer netted against his former club, capitalising on an error in Salzburg's backline and, minutes later, Poulsen rose highest to meet a Kampl cross and set up a stunning finale. However, in the last minute of normal time, Leipzig's momentum was dashed. A Hannes Wolf pass with the back of his heel was finished by substitute Fredrik Gulbrandsen. Salzburg won 3-2 and went 1-0 up in the Red Bull wars.

An excellent watch for the neutral, this fixture perhaps did some good for both clubs in quashing any talk of a potential collusion. Salzburg were rapid, relentless and, even after losing their two-goal lead late in the game, they kept their intensity up. Keen on bettering their semi-final run from the previous season, they were clearly the hungrier of the two sides. Rangnick and Leipzig showed a bit of frustration that they couldn't correct the mistakes they had made in Europe in the previous season, but they had five more chances to make things right.

Ahead of the Germans' next group match against Rosenborg, Rune Bratseth, the former Werder Bremen defender and member of the Norwegian club's board of directors, made his feelings about the absurdity of both Red Bull teams in one group, and competition, clear: 'When I saw the two clubs from Red Bull in our group, I naturally had to think: "Is that allowed?" People should think of when they play against each other and ask what happens when it's the penultimate matchday and maybe they both need a point [to qualify],' he said to *WDR*. 'It's quite clear they work together; you can't call it anything else. You can't get away from this context. If they are right legally [referring to the UEFA decision in 2017], it doesn't mean that it is right morally. From that perspective it is not good.'

On the pitch, Leipzig hit back, as Augustin, Ibrahima Konaté and Matheus Cunha struck to complete a 3-1 win. Over in Austria, Salzburg had a 3-1 success of their own to enjoy over Celtic, with Dabbur's double and Wolf's solitary strike putting them in pole position in the group. In the next round of fixtures, both Red Bull-backed clubs continued their dominance as Salzburg strolled by Rosenborg with a 3-0 win, while Leipzig put two past Celtic without reply. It was in the reverse fixtures where things really started to get heated and the integrity of the competition was called into question once again. Salzburg won 5-2 in Trondheim, but after Celtic's 2-1 win over Leipzig in Glasgow, the race to qualify for the round of 32 intensified. Ahead of the two Red Bull clubs meeting in Austria, there were concerns aplenty from Scotland.

Scottish paper, the *Daily Record*, weren't shy in their reporting just before the clash: 'Are Celtic fans right to fear a Salzburg and Leipzig carve-up?' they asked. 'Because of Leipzig's head-to-head advantage [over Celtic] Celtic must better their rivals' result over the next two games – but there's a palpable sense of concern it could all be in vain.' With Salzburg's perfect record and Leipzig a win away from all but guaranteeing qualification, it was natural to be concerned.

However, Mintzlaff put all conspiracies to rest. Speaking to *Sportbuzzer*, when asked whether there were any orders from Mateschitz, he said: 'Nonsense! Dietrich Mateschitz has zero-point-zero per cent involvement in operations and I also have no influence on Salzburg. Salzburg and Leipzig have a common past, but neither a common present nor a common future. Salzburg itself still needs a point to move forward safely. We have to score points in order to continue in three competitions. Salzburg will certainly be highly motivated to compete against us again. And, of course, we want to do better after the first leg.'

With qualification in mind, Rangnick sent out a stronger side this time around:

[4-2-2-2] Mvogo — Mukiele, Orban, Upamecano, Saracchi
Laimer, Ilsanker — Bruma, Cunha — Werner, Augustin
Substitutes: Gulácsi, Klostermann, Halstenberg, Konaté,
Majetschak, Krauß, Poulsen

Rose and Salzburg, meanwhile, stuck to their strengths:

[4-3-1-2] Walke — Lainer, Ramalho, Pongračić, Ulmer —
Schlager, Samassékou, Junzović — Wolf — Dabbur, Gulbrandsen
Substitutes: Stanković, Todorović, Onguene, Mwepu, Daka,
Prevljak, Minamino

While the first fixture between the pair was attacking, the second was far more reserved. It was Rose's team that was clearly the better of the two, forcing some fine saves from Mvogo and threatening frequently. In the first half, Gulbrandsen's volley was well dealt with and, later in the game, Ilsanker's near-post effort was parried away. The Austrians' pressure paid off, however. It was in the 74th minute that a breakthrough was made. Ulmer set up the hero of the first leg, Gulbrandsen, who scored to claim another Salzburg victory. They had now won five out of five in their group, while for Leipzig, qualification was no longer in their hands and they had to beat Rosenborg and hope Celtic lost to Salzburg if they wanted to go through.

Once again, the conspiracies started, but Salzburg's Freund set the record straight just before his team's match against Celtic: 'Of course we will go full throttle in Glasgow, and we want to win. And if that means we can help the people of Leipzig we will be double happy. We are in a fortunate position where we can enjoy the last game because we have qualified. I know the people of Leipzig are keeping their fingers crossed for us and I hope we can make them pleased with us. But remember, regardless of who we will be helping, we always do our best in every game. And we will do our utmost to win, especially for our fans who have travelled to Scotland. If we could make it six wins out of six, that would be a great achievement and if we can help our friends in Leipzig then great.'

It was all in vain, though. Dabbur and Gulbrandesen's goals earned Salzburg a 2-1 win in Glasgow, making them one of only two clubs along with Eintracht Frankfurt to win all six of their group matches. Although they gave Leipzig some assistance, the Germans still crashed out. Rosenborg's Tore Reginiussen scored a late equaliser which resulted in Leipzig finishing third, two points behind Celtic and out of Europe.

In a dramatic group where the action went beyond the pitch, it was Salzburg who prevailed in the battles within. Featuring emotional returns to former clubs, a few conspiracy theories, criticism of UEFA's approach and two entertaining matches, the first meetings between the two Red Bull clubs in official competition were as modern as modern football can be.

LEARNING BY DOING

AT THE small but picturesque Colovray Stadium in Nyon, Switzerland in late April 2017, Alexander Schmidt made history for Red Bull Salzburg. With the scores level between the Austrians and Benfica in the UEFA Youth League Final, his left foot reached the end of Hannes Wolf's cross in the 75th minute to complete a five-minute comeback in a difficult encounter. Some stern defending, a few missed Benfica chances and 20 minutes later Salzburg won the final, becoming only the third winners in four editions of the competition after Barcelona and back-to-back champions Chelsea. Austrian clubs haven't enjoyed success on the European scene, so this victory, even though it came for a younger age group, was immense.

For Red Bull as a whole, this was one of their masterpieces. It was a reward for years of effort, investment and commitment towards their academy and younger players. Crucial to the victory in Nyon were the years of planning that had gone into it, to make sure their players were coached properly and acquired the right experience out on the pitch. FC Liefering, Salzburg's farm club, are the embodiment of that. The players that started the Youth League Final in Nyon had plenty of experience playing for Liefering, amassing a total of 162 appearances between them in the physically demanding second division of Austrian football. This level of practice is unmatched. The

Youth League is for players who are 19 and under and, at most clubs, players usually play against opposition of their age group with a few sporadic senior appearances. Salzburg's careful structuring and futuristic planning gave them an edge, and the results have been there to see.

Just like all the clubs linked with Red Bull, Liefering were also despised in Austria, with fans feeling that they were challenging the integrity of the Austrian league system. Additionally, the club's formation was just as complicated as it was controversial. Officially founded in 2012 with the same colours, kits and identical crest as Salzburg and Leipzig, albeit without the famous two bulls, their links go back over six decades to 1947. To understand Liefering's foundation, it's worth grasping the Austrian league structure and changes to its regulations in the 21st century.

From 2005 up until 2010, Austrian Bundesliga clubs were allowed to field their reserve teams in the second division. This was something clubs like Salzburg and Austria Wien, amongst others, took advantage of. However, for the 2010/11 season, it was announced that the 2. Liga would be reduced from 12 clubs to 10 and, more strikingly, reserve teams would be prohibited. Salzburg were keen on having a team in the second tier because they wanted to give their players the platform of competitive football and so they began their search for a way to have a team just below the Salzburg senior side. They felt their reserves were too good for the third division, and that was reflected in the performances. In the 2010/11 campaign, the reserves impressively won the Western Regionalliga (one of three levels of the third division along with the Eastern and Central Regionalliga) but weren't eligible for promotion.

It was in that season that they were unofficially tied up with Union Sport-Klub (USK Anif), another third division side who were based in a suburb of Salzburg and were well-established in Austrian football. Salzburg loaned out several of their youngsters to Anif in the hope that they would be promoted. Unfortunately for the Red Bull club, Anif finished third and were not allowed to play in the promotion play-offs, denting Salzburg's plans. It was in that summer of 2011 that Salzburg and Anif tried to establish a formal link, but due to the lack of time before the new season began, a deal never materialised.

The two clubs entered the 2011/12 season as separate entities, but behind the scenes, they were working on a solution that would see Red Bull get what they wanted. By 2012, this is what it came to: USK Anif struck a deal with Red Bull that would see all players from Salzburg's reserve team – known as RB Juniors – move to USK Anif and play in a bigger stadium. In turn, Red Bull formed another club called FC Anif, thus making sure there was still a third-tier team based in Anif. This is where all the original USK Anif players were transferred to. In the 2011/12 campaign, Anif once again missed out on promotion to the second division and that meant the newly founded FC Liefering, who were the rebranded version of USK Anif, would begin life in the third tier in 2012/13. Complicated? Yes.

In a similar way, Salzburg were also tied up with Pasching that season, a club playing in Regionalliga Central (Anif were in Regionalliga West). Pasching had a vast history, playing in the Bundesliga as recently as 2007 until they sold their playing licence to Austria Kärnten. In 2010, Kärnten filed for bankruptcy and, a year later, Pasching were re-formed, starting in the third division. The new Pasching were struggling, which Salzburg recognised, and they loaned them several players as a safety net. Miraculously, they avoided relegation and, just a year later, they were fighting LASK for promotion whilst also amazingly going on to win the ÖFB Cup, even managing to beat Red Bull Salzburg 2-1 in the semi-final at the Red Bull Arena. The plan for Salzburg was to see Liefering win the Regionalliga West and Pasching win the Regionalliga Central, thus guaranteeing that a team associated with them made it to the second division.

Pasching failed to get there, but Liefering did. Over the summer, Red Bull successfully managed to convince the licence board of the Bundesliga that they were a separate club with no formal connections to Liefering, suggesting that they were just a sponsor of the club. The licence was given. As a gesture of goodwill, Liefering offered not to participate in the ÖFB Cup and they refused to exercise the voting rights that are given to clubs in the top two tiers, as well as not being able to earn promotion to the Bundesliga. Back to Pasching, Salzburg continued to support them but only until the end of 2013/14 season, due to the fact that their objective had been achieved by Liefering. Three years later, Pasching became the farm club for LASK, renaming themselves as FC Juniors OÖ and earning promotion to the 2. Liga. In 2018, the second division was reformed again, growing to 16 clubs from 10 and the league allowed three reserve teams to play in it. Salzburg, through Liefering, and LASK, through Pasching, don't have official reserve teams, but other big names such as Austria Wien, Rapid Wien, Innsbruck and Sturm Graz all had their eyes on the second tier.

Liefering's promotion being permitted was not taken well by the others in Austria. A fan initiative called *Fairness im Fußball* (fairness in football) produced a long letter stating OFB and UEFA statutes regarding integrity and called for the licence not to be given: 'We perceive these circumstances as a great distortion of competition, this approach of Red Bull Salzburg in no way promotes the attractiveness of Austrian football and we are sure that this is not in the spirit of Austrian sport.' Mortiz Grobovschek, one of the co-founders of Austria Salzburg (the phoenix club born after Red Bull's takeover in 2005) spoke about his own displeasure over the cooperation to *11Freunde*, just before his team were set to face Liefering in 2013: 'The hope for Austrian football is that at some point in time the entire interest of Red Bull will focus on RB Leipzig. Due to the importance of the German Bundesliga and the correspondingly larger market, Red Bull Salzburg would then degenerate into a single farm team.'

Austrian league regulations also permit a certain number of players to be transferred between Bundesliga clubs and lower league clubs outside of assigned transfer windows. These are known as cooperation players and Salzburg and Liefering take advantage of the rule. They aren't the only ones, however, with the likes of Sturm Graz and LASK making use of it too. From a purely sporting perspective, Liefering is a masterstroke from Red Bull and they are reaping the benefits. Both Salzburg and Leipzig have profited from it and are likely to in the future as well. As mentioned, they help in many ways, such as giving a chance to foreign players to find their feet in European football, giving young players the opportunity to play competitive football against strong opposition and developing stars for the future. Some recent success stories have been Patson Daka, Enock Mwepu and Karim Adeyemi.

Since winning promotion to the second division, Liefering have managed to stay there, showing their quality and constantly challenging the top teams, despite not being eligible for further promotion. In the seven seasons that they have spent in the tier between 2014 and 2020, they have finished third, second, fourth, second, fifth, tenth and third as the players have proven that they want to show their best form to progess in their careers.

Xaver Schlager, who formerly played for Salzburg, Liefering and won the Youth League in 2017 before moving to VfL Wolfsburg in the summer of 2019, tells me: 'It helped me a lot. You come in from the U-18s, which is kids' football – it's not physical. There aren't many tackles, there are no duels. At Liefering, you come into the second division and it is only physical: only long balls, duels, headers. When you're small in size and not strong, you have to be fast, so they don't catch you. There are two objectives for the players at Liefering: the first one is also to become strong and physical and the second is to become faster. For me, I mainly looked at one option because I'm not so fast, so I have to be as strong as the opponents. So, I learned a lot from the physical standpoint. Personally, the one and a half years in the second division with Liefering were maybe the most important [in my career] because you learn from the older players – they are not so fast, but they are clever. You also have to be smart to play against them.'

Schlager was the captain of the Youth League team and he jointly topped the assists charts with five, earning a reputation as one of the best players of the tournament. Also a part of that team were players who are first-team figures now – the likes of Wolf and Amadou Haidara now play for RB Leipzig, while Daka is Jesse Marsch's leading forward for Salzburg. They were led by coach Marco Rose, who is now at Borussia Mönchengladbach. The Leipzig native was always a keen learner and worked his way through the Salzburg academy. His potential as a coach was recognised by Jürgen Klopp, who in 2004 as the manager of Mainz, predicted that his defender would do well on the touchline. Rose's credentials were improved by Salzburg's run in the famed youth competition.

Going into the competition that season, Salzburg were keen on correcting the mistakes of the previous season, when they had lost 4-0 to Roma at home in the play-offs. As a result of the senior team not making the Champions League group stages, Salzburg qualified for the Youth League through the Domestic Champions Path – a play-off consisting of the youth champions of UEFA's member nations, where they beat Kazakhstan's Kairat 9-1 over two legs (this was the only two-legged round in Salzburg's run).

Then, they overcame a Manchester City team including the likes of Jadon Sancho, Brahim Díaz and Tosin Adarabioyo with a bit of luck in a penalty shoot-out. It was Díaz and Paolo Fernandes who missed for the English club to set Salzburg up for another mammoth tie against the previous season's runners-up, Paris Saint-Germain. If people believed they were riding their luck thus far, against PSG, they showed their class. Salzburg thumped the French side 5-0 and, in doing so, received plaudits from the world over.

Schlager says: 'It was very special for us. Austria was not popular [as a football nation]; Red Bull Salzburg was not popular in the football business. For us, we had the tournament and when we played or when we won, we could get recognition, so everybody was focused on the games. We had a good coach with a perfect technique and then we played against these young teams; everybody was motivated against Paris Saint-Germain, Manchester City and more. We were playing against some really big teams, so their motivation was very high. At Liefering, we played physically, and because of that it was much easier for us [in the Youth League]. For the opposition players, it was like kids' football. They didn't know this level of physicality, but we did, so we were stronger. That was the key to our improvement and to playing well. It was a perfect tournament. We didn't know how far we could go, but we went all the way to the end.'

Rose's team illuminated the tournament. With their shrewd pressing, effective use of full-backs and the youngsters' good grasp of tactical information, this team was having fun. In the quarter-finals, Salzburg beat Atlético Madrid 2-1. Wolf, who was in excellent form in front of goal, added to his tally of five with another as Salzburg were spurred on to the last four. Sadly for Schlager, he missed the semi-finals due to injury and the armband went to Sandro Ingolitsch. The defender, who now plays at Austrian club SKN St Pölten, spoke to me in praise of Rose's influence on the team: 'Marco Rose owns a large part of the triumph. He pays great attention to the smallest details of a soccer game and leaves nothing to chance. In every game we were perfectly geared to the opponent. Nevertheless, he always managed to bring a certain looseness and fun to the team. It is not surprising that he is now one of the most exciting coaches in Germany and possibly even in Europe.'

Salzburg were joined by Real Madrid, Benfica and opponents Barcelona to play the two semi-finals and final over four days at the Colovray Stadium in Nyon. The 'Blaugrana', similar to their senior team with their famous possession style, controlled the early parts of the game and turned that domination into a goal – Jordi Mboula ran through the right side and slotted wonderfully into the top corner. As two of the most entertaining teams in the competition, this was always going to be a good match and it lived up to the billing. Keen on hitting back, Salzburg made mistakes in defence but were lucky to not concede. Just after the hour mark, Barcelona were irresponsible and paid the price: Wolf equalised as a result of a bad clearance. Soon after, Daka made amends for missing an open net just minutes earlier by scoring from a cross and setting off on a wild celebration. Wolf was the provider this time and Salzburg were in the final.

Against Benfica for the trophy, Salzburg had to come from behind once again. After going down 1-0 in the first half, they brought Daka off the bench to equalise from a corner, before Schmidt's winner. Ingolistch said of the victory in Nyon: 'All games were special moments, but especially the final four in Nyon is one of my highlights. In the semi-final as well as in the final, we were able to come back and it showed the mentality we had. We only changed small details in order to put more pressure on the opponent. But despite the backlog, we tried to trust our plan because we were convinced that we would still win the game. We were able to turn the game against Barcelona and that gave us strength to win the final as well.' He continued, on the subject of his personal takeaway from the experience: 'Victory in the Youth League is something that I will never forget. The victories against top international clubs such as Manchester City, Atlético Madrid and Barcelona showed the quality of the team at that time. Nobody can take these experiences away from me and they still shape me today.'

The Youth League win was the pinnacle for Liefering and Red Bull. It boosted the reputation of their football operations immensely, giving more credibility and opening pathways for more young players to join in the future. The influence of Liefering should not be understated – had it not been for their presence, many of these players would not have had the opportunity to prove themselves against tough domestic opposition. This experience gave the youngsters an edge on the European scene as well as a solid mentality and it gave the coaches chances at the top level. Liefering is an example of Red Bull's careful planning, and the Youth League was the perfect reward.

CREATING A LEGACY

IN RED Bull's football empire, names such as Ralf Rangnick, Paul Mitchell and Jesse Marsch are often praised for their influence on the company's football operations, but one person who has largely gone under the radar despite his many contributions is Ernst Tanner. Now working at MLS's Philadelphia Union as their sporting director, the German spent six years at Red Bull Salzburg, joining with Rangnick in 2012 before departing for the United States of America in 2018, having left an incredible legacy behind for his successors to build on.

I had the pleasure of speaking to Tanner, and listening to his knowledge and experiences in the game was most certainly illuminating. In his own words, this is his background in the game: 'I started as a sports scientist. I played football until I was 26 at a professional level in the third division in Germany in parallel to my studies. My entry into coaching came at youth level at 1860 Munich. Here, I soon grew to the academy director role. I was there for about 15 years. We had been very successful with our youth development – in these 15 years, I think we brought out more than 70 professional players and were well known throughout Germany for our youth development. Then, in 2009, I went to Hoffenheim where I also started as an academy director but, after ten months, I got the sporting director role. After three years at Hoffenheim, I went to Red Bull in August 2012.'

Known as Munich's other club, 1860 are one of the most prominent in youth development in Germany with the likes of Sven Bender, Lars Bender and Kevin Volland all making their way through the system whilst Tanner was there. His move to Hoffenheim in 2009 was in the middle of Rangnick's five-year stint as head coach, between 2006 and 2011, during which the Sinsheim club went from the third division to the Bundesliga with a philosophy that involved improving unpolished youngsters. Considering Tanner's success at both clubs, it comes as no surprise that Rangnick took him to Red Bull and asked him to oversee the academy in Salzburg, along with some other responsibilities.

On his role in Austria, he says: 'I was the academy director. It was a big project, as in the beginning there was an academy and there was a new project coming up with Liefering, so that was what really attracted me because I saw the opportunities. In the beginning, I was also responsible for recruitment and, as I did the same at Hoffenheim, I was, more or less, establishing the recruitment – at that time we did it together with Leipzig because it was allowed back then. Later, I became responsible for Africa and establishing our recruitment network there.

'I was, in a way, quite influential. I was the guy with the most experience, probably behind Ralf Rangnick, of course, who took me with him, and we did a restructuring of the youth department there. We implemented our new philosophy and playing style. We put a real focus on innovative things. As it was in an academy, we had the chance to try things out without any consequences – if it didn't work out, we could learn. I liked that role very much as I was in the background but was also having some influence even on the transfers of the first team – that was a very good time.'

Austria's standing in international football has not been the greatest. The nation hasn't won a game at a major tournament since Italia '90, and even that was a dead rubber match against the USA after both nations had already been knocked out. They've played at one World Cup and two editions of the European Championships since then (one of which they co-hosted in 2008), failing to impress in all. Even for the domestic clubs, success on the Continental stage has been rare. Now, however, they seem to be in a good position and Tanner highlights that the changes Salzburg implemented were crucial to this resurgence.

'I would say the culture we established at Salzburg was important. There was a real collaboration with every part inside the club and you could really feel that there was a lot of focus on our young players. There was a pathway for them. We were discussing things closely together with the professional side – that's very seldom for clubs that you are so close together and that the youth gets so much respect. In addition to that, of course, we had the perfect development and we did good scouting. In time, we got a good reputation which led to better players joining. It was quite easy.'

It's not controversial to suggest that Salzburg's academy is one of the finest in Europe, right on the level of esteemed outfits such as Benfica, Barcelona and Real Madrid. Their success combined with the accolades and standing of their alumni is enough justification for that. Key to the consistency is a routine and, without revealing too many secrets, Tanner provides a little insight into what the players were put through in an average week at their cutting-edge facility: 'We trained six times a week and, alongside that, they had to go to school, so the players had to wake up between six and seven in the morning. Two times per week, they had morning training and then they went to school and came back home, did some homework before training again, followed by some individual workout between meals. They had maybe one to one-and-a-half hours of spare time in the evening during the week and during the weekends they would play a game. They would often get one day off per week.'

The fruit of their labour was, of course, winning the UEFA Youth League in 2017. As mentioned previously, Salzburg were the perennial entertainers of that competition, scoring 29 goals across seven matches and beating Benfica in the final. For Tanner, that victory was about character and the way they achieved their results was evidence of that. Tanner was the person who had overseen Salzburg's move to their modern academy; he was the one who implemented their innovative playing philosophy and winning Europe's most prestigious youth competition was sweetest for him. After failure in the previous year, going all the way brought pure satisfaction.

'Austria, and in particular Salzburg, is not the most famous ground for developing or growing young players. We had a chance in the Youth League before when we played AS Roma and we had a terrible experience [in the previous season]. They were not that much better than us in a way. In terms of chances we were quite equal. The initial point [where we felt we could win in 2017] was when we dominated Manchester City, but despite that, we beat them on penalties. We were far better than them and should've won the game in normal time. Sometimes, you have these initial moments when you do something no one expected you to do and that game was it for us. We were even behind in the shoot-out, but then they missed, and we got lucky before winning. That gave us a lot of confidence and then we beat Paris Saint-Germain, Atlético Madrid and all these big clubs.'

He continues: 'Nobody was expecting Salzburg to win all these games and compete against these big players in youth football. That was amazing. We had that feeling that now we were really there and not only can we compete, but we can also beat the best. We came from behind in the semi-final and final, coming back from 1-0 down and it was difficult to turn the game, but it showed a lot about the character and the mentality of the whole team as well as the coaches. That was really satisfying for us, after all the work we had put in.'

It's worth remembering that while Red Bull Salzburg were winning trophies prior to Rangnick's arrival in 2012, there wasn't a clear structure in place for the future of the club. The German's arrival and revolutionary youth-centred approach didn't appeal to the fans initially, but as the supporters subsequently recognised that they had an identity to be proud of, they warmed to the changes.

Tanner says: 'Red Bull was not respected at all when we were starting off – not even in Austria. Formerly, they bought ageing stars and, when we arrived, Ralf turned it around and for the first team, so we started signing younger players who were not very well-known. This was something the fans were not used to, they felt like it was a punch in their face. Eventually, the interest started to grow. When you see the number of fans at our Youth League home games that year, you can see the difference. Against Atlético Madrid, [the last home game before the last four in Nyon] we had about 5,700 people in the stadium, which was more than the first team had in the following week. You could see that there was an acceptance growing from the local people for what we were doing and that was probably the most satisfying thing.'

The Red Bull way of dictating the game without the ball, using numerical superiority, quick transitions and winning the ball back with aggressive pressing is taught throughout all age groups and Tanner believes that was vital in winning the Youth League. He recalls the semi-final against Barcelona as the epitome of their model: 'We played differently. That's something many people are learning out of their experiences in life: if you do things differently, you can be successful and that was absolutely true in the Youth League when we won. Nobody could cope with our style. I remember the game against Barcelona – they played some fantastic football; their style of play was very good, but they couldn't live with our pressure. We constantly attacked them, and their coaches couldn't adapt to what we were doing. They weren't flexible enough. They tried to play it out from that back all the time and we were constantly attacking their defences as well as their goalkeeper and that led to chance after chance for us. They got insecure in a way, and we were able to turn the game. It was a clash of cultures, and we were able to get the win.'

Tanner also has good memories of the coach, Marco Rose. The former defender, who ended his playing days in 2010 after representing Mainz for eight years, was appointed as the head coach of hometown club Lokomotive Leipzig in the Regionalliga Nordost (the fourth tier). Rose started his playing career at that club in 1995, back when they were known as VfB Leipzig; however, his coaching stint lasted just one season as Salzburg's youth teams came calling. It was Tanner who gave him the job, and he looks back on that time with some laughter.

'The story of his appointment is funny. I got the name from an agent, and then I did some research and found out that he played under Ralf [when they were both at Hannover 96 between 2001 and 2002]. I told him: "Hey Ralf, there is a coach who is believed to be quite good. We are looking for an U-16 coach and he might be right for the job," and Ralf replied to me: "Ah! He was my player. I could've had that thought myself!" He contacted him immediately after that and we were lucky to get him.'

On Rose's career at Salzburg, Tanner adds: 'He had never worked in youth football before so he would need to adapt. U-16 is something different to what he had done so far, and he was leaving the professional level so he would need time. The academy was the right place for him – the discussions with other coaches, the exchanging of experiences in youth football and the education we were giving probably helped him a lot. He would do the coaching Pro Licence within the next year and then we promoted him to the U-18s. Even after that, when Óscar Garcia [first-team head coach] left the first team, he had already signed up for another year with the U-18s, but after Garcia left, we thought the time was right to promote Rose to the first team.'

Rose's assistant throughout his Salzburg days and even now at Borussia Mönchengladbach is René Marić. Still only 28, Marić is one of the most interesting coaches in football. He formerly played and coached his local team, TSU Handenberg in Austria, but his tactical writings on the German blog *Spielverlagerung.de* really caught the eye. The depth of his analysis led to the likes of Thomas Tuchel as well as clubs such as Midtjylland and Brentford calling for his assistance as they wanted players and teams analysed. The articles may have been complex for the standard fan, but coaches appreciated them and Tanner hysterically recalls his appointment in 2017.

'That was also quite a funny story. René was one of the writers on the website, *Spielverlagerung*. We were always very curious because there was somebody out there who really analysed our U-18 games in an almost perfect way. The signature under his articles were always his initials, "RM", and we were wondering at the club if Marco Rose was doing his own analysis on a website because he has the same initials as René Marić if you turn it around. Eventually, we found out who it was and that was the reason for getting in touch with him. Of course, after that, we decided to sign him up because the knowledge and talent was visible. We always wanted to have Austrian or local coaches. As it is known, there isn't that much quality in terms of coaching.'

Learning by doing is a theory often associated with Salzburg, and there is no better example of that than Liefering. I asked Tanner about what they contributed to the Red Bull model, and his response was firm: 'A lot. They are very important. All the development we were doing would not have been very helpful if we weren't able to put it in action in an appropriate style and that is exactly the purpose Liefering serves. In addition to that, the league regulations in Austria allow us to bring in a reasonable number of foreign players, and that was our focus so we could play them there [at Liefering] and cultivate them there. The players are allowed to make mistakes there in order to learn from them. So, I think that Liefering are an example of the right things we were doing.'

Tanner's influence goes beyond just Salzburg – he has made a slight contribution to the current RB Leipzig team as well. Their head coach, Julian Nagelsmann, was one of many protégé's of Tanner. It was at 1860 Munich where they first met and, while it is known that Nagelsmann was at Hoffenheim whilst Rangnick was the head coach of the first team, it was Tanner who he worked closely with and the young manager's success and intelligence does not surprise his mentor.

'He was a player of mine at 1860 Munich and his career ended quite frustratingly because he was injured very often. We used to joke, calling him "glass bones" because once he did anything, something broke. But he was always intelligent, and he was a student of these high-performance schools. We always had the idea that he could be a coach because of that. As a player, he was always very strategic as well. He started as an assistant under Alexander Schmidt at 1860 Munich's youth teams. We could see that he was really talented and that is why I appointed him at Hoffenheim for our U-16s. From there, he made his way.'

The experienced German academy director left his role at Salzburg in 2018, stating that he wanted a new challenge. In moving to Philadelphia, Tanner rejected opportunities in his home country as well as China, where he was offered a hefty pay package. Looking back, he is proud of his time in Austria and, more than the trophies, it was the image he helped create during his six-year spell at the club that he is most proud of.

'There are so many things we are proud of apart from the Youth League. We won many domestic titles and numerous high-quality international tournaments, but I think the biggest achievement is that we created and took care of an incredible reputation for Salzburg in European football. At one point in time, if you met anyone and told them you were working for Salzburg, you would get a lot of respect and there were times when we won the Youth League and were successful in the Europa League, everybody was trying to emulate our system. It's still the case right now that people call me and there is a high demand for the coaches who worked at Salzburg as well. People often want to know about our system, the model, our coaches, the education – everything! That is probably the biggest achievement that we had: we made Salzburg famous on the European football scene.'

As we approach the end of our conversation, I ask Tanner how far he believes Salzburg can go in European football: 'They have been going so far that I would say that what they achieved in the Champions League and these spectacular games against Liverpool and others, is the maximum they can do. Certainly, if everything goes well, they could win the Europa League because we were very close in 2018, when we were knocked out by Marseille in the semi-final – that was perhaps unlucky with a few decisions by the referee, but if we had won that, we would have been a better opponent for Atlético Madrid in the final. Maybe they could win it one day. But this is a question that nobody can give you the right answer for.'

Tanner's role in Red Bull's football machine may be underappreciated outside Austria, but there is no denying that he was a mightily influential figure. His ability to identify the right minds and work with others helped make Salzburg one of the most esteemed clubs in Europe. The positive effects of his efforts have been seen, and will only continue in the future.

SPREADING THEIR WINGS

VALENCIA, SHAKHTAR Donetsk, Maccabi Haifa, Hapoel Tel Aviv, Dudelange, Fenerbahçe, Malmö, Malmö (again), Dinamo Zagreb, Rijeka and Red Star. Eleven times Red Bull Salzburg attempted to qualify for the group stages of the Champions League between 2006 and 2018, 11 times they fell in the qualifying rounds. It wasn't until 2019, which included Liverpool and Tottenham, second and fourth in the Premier League, squaring off in the Champions League Final as well as Austria's UEFA club coefficient ranking rising up to 11th, that Salzburg were able to make it to the competition proper of Europe's top club tournament. While a record like that may reflect badly, it's worth mentioning that since Red Bull's takeover, Salzburg have been Austria's most dominant club – and by some distance.

The lack of Champions League football and the manner in which they failed to get there was certainly hurtful. Losing to Luxembourg's Dudelange was shocking; making the same mistakes twice in consecutive years against Malmö was hard to believe and falling to Red Star on away goals despite going two up at home in the second leg raised questions about the mentality around the club.

Despite their Champions League disappointment, Austria's rise to 11th in the club coefficient rankings is mostly down to Salzburg – their efforts in the Europa League are commendable.

Since Ralf Rangnick was given the keys to unlock Red Bull's potential, tough decisions had been made, but they all played a part in refining the club and there have been times when Salzburg have been a respected outfit on the European scene for their neat football. Ricardo Moniz, the Dutch coach on the Salzburg bench before Rangnick's arrival, left in confusing circumstances in the summer of 2012 and his replacement wasn't the most exciting. Rangnick, however, knew what he was doing and put full faith in his man.

At the time of the German's arrival, Salzburg had won four out of the previous six league titles, so continuing that success was of paramount importance. However, the appointment of his compatriot Roger Schmidt as head coach was underwhelming – not many people knew who he was. Schmidt's entry into coaching and career until that point had been full of perseverance. It wasn't in his plans to be a full-time coach and at the start of the 21st century; Schmidt was working at Benteler, a company that supplied parts to car manufacturers. His career in the lower leagues as a player concluded and he would slowly transition into coaching, taking the reins of sixth-tier Delbrücker whilst carrying out his job with the conglomerate. Promotion up one division followed and, in 2007, the coach left both his day job and Delbrücker and moved to another fifth division team, Preußen Münster. There, he would spur them upwards, winning another promotion in his first season whilst also winning two regional cups to qualify for the DFB Pokal.

In 2010, Schmidt was on the move again after Preußen Münster couldn't move up to 3. Liga and the German then progressed to getting his UEFA Pro Licence. A year later, he returned to management, this time with Paderborn, a city and club he had a great connection with. It was here that he had picked up his mechanical engineering degree some two decades prior and he had even played for the team at a semiprofessional level in 2002. Nine years later, he was their coach and a grand fifth-place finish in 2. Bundesliga as well his pressing philosophy garnered the attention of Rangnick, who appointed him at Salzburg. Schmidt's initial weeks in Austria didn't do him any favours. He was appointed as head coach in mid June. A month later, the shock against Dudelange took place and his team were knocked out of the Champions League in the second qualifying round. The Luxembourgers had gone through on away goals after losing the first leg 4-3.

The defeat in the Champions League may have been disheartening, but this season was one for new figures to settle in and establish Salzburg's identity. Schmidt needed time and so did Rangnick. That summer, the Austrians brought in two new players who would be vital to them in the coming years, Sadio Mané and Kevin Kampl, as the staff made use of their far-reaching links. A crucial objective of the team was to let go of the older names and bring in younger, fresher talent. Salzburg fans were accustomed to winning silverware, but this season wouldn't bring any. Schmidt's philosophy revolved around pressing, and implementing that was imperative for the long-term future. With a young squad that featured players such as Jonathan Soriano and Martin Hinteregger along with the two aforementioned signings, the coach fielded a 4-4-2 that would often convert to a 4-2-2-2 and it made the team very exciting. They scored a mammoth 91 goals in 36 league games, but only finished second as too many draws gave Austria Wien the title.

Nevertheless, the fans were now on board with the project and the glory would soon follow. In the next season, Salzburg fell to Fenerbahçe in the third qualifying round of the Champions League, but elsewhere, they were unstoppable. Key to their pressing were the two forwards, Soriano and Alan, who troubled the opposition defences relentlessly – *angriffpressing* – as it's known. The team were labelled as a pressing machine and in training Schmidt used a clock that would ring every five seconds if the attackers hadn't won the ball back after losing it. Goals came at a constant rate too; by the end of the 2013/14 season, Salzburg had scored 110 and they had won the league by 23 March 2014 – nearly two months before the season ended. They even beat St Pölten in the final of the ÖFB Cup.

It was in the Europa League that Schmidt and Salzburg's stock rose. They posted a 100 per cent record in the group stages and against Ajax in the round of 32, Salzburg won 6-1 on aggregate. In the first leg of that tie away from home, a 3-0 win, their intensity was unmatched, and this was the pinnacle of the Schmidt era. Such was their quality that even Pep Guardiola, then of Bayern Munich, was astounded when the two teams met in a mid-season friendly which the Austrians won 3-0; he claimed he had never seen a team play with such intensity. Back in the Europa League, Salzburg were knocked out in the round of 16 by Basel and, by the end of the season, the same Schmidt that no one had had an idea of at the start of his tenure was now being pleaded with not to leave. The fans wanted him for the long run.

However, the German returned home, moving to Bayer Leverkusen. Under Schmidt, the Salzburg team had played some wonderful attacking football and the front four of Mané, Kampl, Soriano and Alan was exhilarating, but it could also be said that the team's balance was affected, and that was evident against Basel. Take nothing away from the stint, though. It was a massive success for the club and coach. Replacing him was Adi Hütter, who was a legend in these parts. The Austrian formerly played for Austria Salzburg, and even scored the winner against Eintracht Frankfurt in the first leg of the 1994 UEFA Cup quarter-finals – a season where Salzburg reached the final but lost to Inter. For an Austrian team, there is no better feeling than beating a German club in Europe and, for his contribution to a wonderful era, Hütter was a revered figure.

Back in 2008, Hütter had been in charge of Salzburg's junior team – his first coaching venture – and a record of 13 wins in 35 wasn't the most eye-catching, but it was something to build on. A year later, he took over at second division Altach, who had recently been relegated from the top flight. Three seasons and three near-misses in the hunt for promotion did Hütter's reputation some good as he stabilised a falling club, but it ended in a strange manner – with him departing for Grödig, another second-division team. There was belief that he could take Altach back up, so to see him move lower down the table and start from scratch raised eyebrows. However, he would prove the doubters wrong. In his first season, his team finished first, ten points clear of Altach, while in his second, Grödig surprisingly claimed third in the Bundesliga, behind Red Bull Salzburg and Rapid Wien. In two years, Hütter established himself as Austria's brightest coach.

Given his history with the club and achievements with Grödig, it was only right that Hütter got the Salzburg job. The start wasn't easy and losing players was as frustrating for him as it was for the supporters. Mané left for Southampton on a sour note, while Kampl and Alan would depart in the winter, moving to Borussia Dortmund and Guangzhou Evergrande. Additionally, just like his predecessor, Hütter was thrown into the firing line early on. After beating Qarabağ in the third qualifying round of the Champions League, hope was raised that 2014 could finally be Salzburg's year, but then they drew Malmö in the play-offs and bowed out. But, once again, just like for his predecessor, the Champions League sadness didn't spoil their season.

Hütter also favoured the high-tempo, high-pressing 4-4-2 and he made the best use of the players he had at his disposal. Soriano, the talismanic forward who kept getting better, was at his best, providing a remarkable 46 goals and 20 assists in all competitions as he made full use of the coach's desire for relentlessness in attack. Alongside him was Marcel Sabitzer, who joined on loan from the cousins in Leipzig – he contributed 27 goals and 21 assists in all competitions. It was evident from the start that this team was full of thrills: in

Hütter's debut league game, they walloped Rapid Wien 6-1, with their energy proving to be difficult to cope with. A tough patch in the middle of the campaign didn't trouble them as it was clear Salzburg were levels above the rest in terms of talent and coaching. Even in Europe, they were untouchable in the group stages, topping their Europa League group consisting of Celtic, Dinamo Zagreb and Astra Giurgiu. After losing key players in the winter, though, they would fall to Villarreal in the round of 32.

The promise was still there domestically, and Salzburg were on course for another double. In the last eight and the last four of the cup, Salzburg came up against two of Hütter's former clubs: Altach and Grödig, beating them 4-0 and 2-0 respectively, while in the final, Austria Wien were dispatched 2-0 after an additional 30 minutes. Goalkeeper Péter Gulácsi was sent off in that game. The league was won, although without the same superiority of the previous year. A tally of 99 goals was a testament to the team's attacking prowess. The silverware, along with the football, was helpful for Hütter's reputation, but he was not keen on the way things were done over the course of the season. Losing his best players was frustrating and, although Salzburg viewed him as the man to carry them forward for the next few years, he looked in a different direction, leaving his role after a solitary, successful campaign. Hütter didn't want to be at a feeder club and Salzburg's activity in the summer that followed perhaps justified his departure. Gulácsi, André Ramalho and Stefan Ilsanker – mainstays in the first team in this successful period under two managers – left, while Hinteregger departed in the winter. The player turnover was not appreciated.

Replacing Hütter would prove to be a challenge. Peter Zeidler, the former Hoffenheim assistant to Rangnick and the Liefering coach was promoted to the first team. Bad results, including elimination from both the European competitions before the group stages, as well as inconsistent league form, proved to be his end. He was gone by December 2015. By the end of that month, Óscar García, the former Barcelona man who had been wanted by the club in the summer, was given the reins.

Over the next season and a half under García, Salzburg won the double, whilst their Europa League campaigns weren't as expected – they went out in the group stages in 2016/17. Four years after Rangnick's arrival and the improvement in talent was significant. Gone were the days of older, expensive players and in came elite youngsters such as Naby Keïta, Dayot Upamecano, Takumi Minamino, Diadie Samassékou, Konrad Laimer and Hwang Hee-chan. Rangnick's changes were a slow-burning, rather than overnight, revolution and Salzburg wanted to get the best out of their young group. Domestic success alone was not enough, and after the U-19s won the Youth League in 2017, the seniors felt they could go far as well. García was gone and replacing him would be Marco Rose, the Youth League-winning coach.

Of all their coaches since 2012, Rose was arguably the most impressive and his staff were interesting as well. René Marić, the psychologist and tactics fox had an intriguing background; Patrick Eibenberger is a smart fitness coach and an orator of a fine TEDx speech in Innsbruck which explained a bit about his thinking – he ensured the team's fitness levels were always high; René Aufhauser was a good supplement to them all as his analysis of the opposition was always detailed. The trio behind Rose were young as well and this would prove to be inspired. Raphael Honigstein's book, *Das Reboot: How German Football Reinvented Itself and Conquered the World*, highlights that German clubs often appoint young academy coaches for first-team roles because they are able to empathise with and relate better to younger players – an identical approach was deployed here. Despite the team lacking experience, the balance was perfect.

Often fielding a 4-3-1-2, the diamond in midfield was flexible and the biggest beneficiary was the constantly improving Xaver Schlager. The Austrian had the skill and freedom to express himself, playing in a variety of positions in the middle of the park. In front of him was forward Moanes Dabbur, who had taken over from the departed Soriano as the team's goalscorer-in-chief. At the back, Ramalho returned in the winter and became the operator from defence. His presence was vital as Rose emphasised verticality and making use of the possession they had. The speed of the team came from quick passes and direct balls to create scoring chances. In the process, they rarely but effectively made use of their full-backs, and were enjoyable to watch, nonetheless.

The trend of tough starts for new coaches continued as Salzburg fell to Rijeka in the Champions League. However, this was seen as an opportunity and, in the Europa League, Rose's star shone most brightly. After disappointing displays in the two previous years, they topped a group consisting of Marseille, Vitória and Konyaspor. The achievements after that were astounding. In the round of 32, Salzburg beat Real Sociedad, with some late heroics by Minamino at San Sebastián. Then, in the last 16 against a fancied Borussia Dortmund, the Austrians won 2-1 courtesy of Valon Berisha's double and that advantage was defended at home. This was now Salzburg's best European display since they had reached the final of the UEFA Cup in 1994, and it would only get better.

Against Lazio in the quarter-finals, they lost 4-2 in Rome and after Ciro Immobile scored the opener in the 55th minute at the Red Bull Arena a week later, many lost hope. But that was when they kicked into a different gear: 5-2 down on aggregate didn't trouble Salzburg. Immediately, Dabour got one back with the help of a big deflection and then came the barrage. Minute 72: Amadou Haidara scored a stunning long-range goal. Minute 74: Hwang beat the offside trap and then the goalkeeper on the near post. Minute 76: the tie was won as Stefan Lainer headed in a corner. In five minutes, Salzburg won one of the greatest Europa League ties ever and moved on to the semi-finals.

Schlager has fond memories of that run: 'There were so many nice games and the whole year was unbelievable. It started with the Champions League qualification which was not nice. This was very hard for us because we were a much better team. We were knocked out by Red Star and then we focused on the Europa League. We wanted to push ourselves there and it was unbelievable. The first objective was that we wanted to qualify for the round of 16. The most special moment was against Lazio in the second leg. We lost the first game 4-2 and then we were 1-0 down at home. Fifty-five minutes were played and it was very difficult.

'But we thought we still had a chance and maybe we can win. We looked good in the game and then it happened: in five minutes we scored three times and that was unbelievable. The whole stadium gave us so much energy. The people that supported us were amazing and for both the players and fans, that evening was incredible. For me, it was one of the most important games of my career because now I know I can win every game. You only need five minutes, so in every situation you can change the game, and this was great to experience.'

Sadly, that run came to an end against Marseille in the last four. After losing 2-0 at the Vélodrome, Salzburg levelled things up at home before a controversial Marseille goal in extra time sent the Austrians packing. Rose's team conceded from a corner that should never have been given and it left a bitter taste. Despite that, and a defeat in the cup final to Sturm Graz, the league win and Europa League run made this a celebrated campaign.

For an Austrian club to go that far is a difficult feat and repeating it would be even harder. Over the summer, more players moved on: Dabour, Duje Ćaleta-Car, Haidara and Hannes Wolf being the notable ones. The heart-breaking defeat to Red Star would follow, but a 100 per cent record in the Europa League group stages in the following season raised belief that lightening could strike twice. Napoli, however, had other plans in the round of 16. Rose and Salzburg would right the wrongs of the previous year domestically by winning the double – losing just twice all season. Such was their dominance in the cup that by their 2019 win in the final, Salzburg had won 39 out of their previous 41 cup matches (95.12 per cent) – a run stretching all the way back to 2011.

Schlager highlights Rose's impact, saying: 'I think he's a very good coach and his personality is very good. I have had so many coaches in my career that have had an influence and he's also one of them. He taught me a lot of technical things: how to position myself in the game, on the field and to look for my team-mates, at where they go, and [he] told me what to do in those situations. The whole staff was great. We had a good assistant trainer, a good athletic trainer, a good physio. There was the right chemistry in the whole team. We were all just like friends and we wanted to improve. We had one target, one goal: we want to win. Everybody was pushing themselves and we set targets: how can we improve and compare? There was a good atmosphere in the team and in the whole club.' Rose departed for Borussia Mönchengladbach in 2019.

Although results haven't been as favourable in the Champions League, Salzburg's success in the Europa League as well as their dynasty in Austria is a testament to their management. It defines Red Bull's football operations in a nutshell: entertaining football, emphasis on youth – not just in players, but in coaches as well – and an efficient, self-sustainable management. Mistakes are made, as with everything and everyone, but there is still a high level of control and efficiency across all clubs associated with the energy drinks company. This is the Red Bull football empire, and they're just getting started.

Reference:
Honigstein, R., *Das Reboot: How German Football Reinvented Itself and Conquered the World*, Yellow Jersey Press, September 2015

MANY THANKS TO THE FOLLOWING NEWSPAPERS, MAGAZINES AND ONLINE SOURCES

11Freunde
90Minuten
Abseits
Bild
Bundesliga Fanatic
Bundesliga.com
COPA90
CNN
Daily Mail
Der Spiegel
Die Tageszeitung
DW
ESPN
Frankfurter Allgemeine Zeitung
Financial Times
Forbes
Football Paradise
FourFourTwo
Get Football News Germany
Globo Esporte
Goal
LAOLA1

MetroFanatic
RB Live
Red Bull Hub
Reuters
Rotebrausblogger
Sky Sport Austria
Spielverlagerung
Sportbuzzer
Tagesspeigel
The Athletic
The Blizzard
The Economist
The Guardian
The Independent
The New York Times
The Set Pieces
The Daily Telegraph
These Football Times
Tifo Football
Transfermarkt
UEFA.com
WELT
When Saturday Comes
Wired

BOOKS, PODCASTS
AND DOCUSERIES

Football Today, podcast by Jon Mackenzie and Josh
Schneider-Weiler
The Other Bundesliga, podcast by Lee Wingate, Simon Clark
and Tom Middler
*Das Reboot: How German Football Reinvented Itself and
Conquered the World*, by Raphael Honigstein
Mensch: Beyond the Cones, by Jonathan Harding
The European Game: The Secrets of European Football Success, by
Daniel Fieldsend
Formula 1: Drive to Survive, Netflix